Luc Boudreaux
doguedebordeauxsurvival.com

DEPARTMENT OF THE NAVY
Headquarters United States Marine Corps
Washington, D.C. 20350-3000

4 April 2018

CHANGE 1 to MCWP 3-05
Marine Corps Special Operations

1. This publication has been edited to ensure gender neutrality of all applicable and appropriate terms, except those terms governed by higher authority. No other content has been affected.

2. File this transmittal sheet in the front of this publication.

Reviewed and approved this date.

BY DIRECTION OF THE COMMANDANT OF THE MARINE CORPS

Robert S. Walsh

ROBERT S. WALSH
Lieutenant General, U.S. Marine Corps
Deputy Commandant for Combat Development and Integration

Publication Control Numbers:
Publication: 143 000178 00
Change: 143 000178 01

This Page Intentionally Left Blank

DEPARTMENT OF THE NAVY
Headquarters United States Marine Corps
Washington, D.C. 20350-3000

1 June 2017

FOREWORD

The purpose of the Marine Corps Warfighting Publication (MCWP) 3-05, *Marine Corps Special Operations*, is to establish doctrine for the Marine Corps' participation in special operations, specifically the Service's contribution to the United States Special Operations Command with the Marine Forces Special Operations Command (MARFORSOC). This publication is intended for officers, enlisted, and other personnel who are involved with the planning, execution, or support of special operations. It is also designed to assist the joint and interagency community with integrating Marine Corps special operations units into all other planning and operations.

Describing the component at all levels of command, MCWP 3-05 defines the organization, mission, special operations activities, characteristics, command and control, logistics, Marine special operations forces (MARSOF) and Marine air-ground task force interoperability and interdependence, and those methodologies and philosophies unique to special operations.

The Marine Corps' association with special operations requires Marines to understand these operations, including the similarities, differences, and uniqueness of MARSOF with other special operations forces. This publication enhances our understanding of MARSOF and provides both a historical and contemporary look at how the Marine Corps and special operations forces have been interfaced. It is not merely a look at MARFORSOC, but a look at the Marine Corps' role in special operations and special operations forces' role in Marine Corps operations.

Reviewed and approved this date.

BY DIRECTION OF THE COMMANDANT OF THE MARINE CORPS

ROBERT S. WALSH
Lieutenant General, U.S. Marine Corps
Deputy Commandant for Combat
Development and Integration

C. E. MUNDY III
Major General, U.S. Marine Corps
Commander Marine Corps Forces
Special Operations Command

Publication Control Number: 143 000178 00

This Page Intentionally Left Blank

TABLE OF CONTENTS

Chapter 1. Evolution of Marine Corps Special Operations

Chapter 2. Special Operations Fundamentals

Chapter 3. Marine Special Operations Forces Characteristics

Chapter 4. Marine Forces Special Operations Command Organization

Chapter 5. Marine Forces Special Operations Command Command and Control

Chapter 6. Marine Forces Special Operations Command Logistics

Chapter 7. Marine Forces Special Operations Command Training and Education

Chapter 8. Marine Forces Special Operations Command and Marine Air-Ground Task Force Interoperability and Interdependence

Chapter 9. Marine Forces Special Operations Command Preservation of the Force and Family

Appendix A. Assessments

Glossary

References and Related Publications

To Our Reader

CHAPTER 1
EVOLUTION OF MARINE CORPS SPECIAL OPERATIONS

The United States Marines Corps has a rich history filled with expeditionary operations and irregular warfare accomplishments, which provides the foundation for Marine Corps Special Operations. Although the United States Marine Corps (USMC) did not provide a Service component to the United States Special Operations Command (USSOCOM) until 2005, the Marine Corps' ability to conduct and support special operations is demonstrated throughout its history.

In 1805, Lieutenant Presley O'Bannon led a small contingent of Marines on a 600-mile expedition from Alexandria, Egypt, to Derna, Tripoli. Accompanied by an army comprised of Arabs, Europeans, and Greek mercenaries, the 45-day expedition culminated with an attack on a fort occupied by Barbary pirates. Lieutenant O'Bannon's force seized the fort and repelled a counterattack. The enemy was driven from Derna, restoring allegiance to Prince Hamet Karamanli, brother of the ruling Pasha to Tripoli.

The special operations and activities conducted today have direct parallels to the Marine Corps' early, small-scale engagements that had sensitive political considerations. The period described as the "Banana Wars" spanned 1899 to 1934, covering operations in the Philippines, Nicaragua, Haiti, and the Dominican Republic (see fig. 1-1 on page 1-2). These contingencies required a force with the ability to apply an irregular approach to warfare. The Marines quickly became capable of combating a guerilla force, conducting counterinsurgency (COIN), supporting partisan forces, and other nonstandard engagements. The lessons learned marked a significant deviation from traditional warfare and provided an irregular capability for the expeditionary force.

The experiences gathered in "small wars" prompted the Marine Corps to begin systematically analyzing the character and requirements of operations short of war. As a result, the *Small Wars Manual* was published in 1940, establishing a methodology for such operations.

> *Note:* The *Small Wars Manual* is published as a Marine Corps historical publication, Fleet Marine Reference Publication 12-15.

The complex global environment preceding the Japanese attack on Pearl Harbor in 1941 prompted US political and military leadership to consider the development of commando-type units that would assist the Allies in stemming the continued successes of the Axis by conducting clandestine operations. The appropriate use of the specialized, commando-type units produced strategic results and greatly contributed to the Allied victory of World War II.

Figure 1-1. US Marines displaying a captured flag after capturing Augusto Cesar Sandino's headquarters in Poteca, Nicaragua, 1932.

World War II also provided many valuable lessons learned and experience for those Marines who served in the Office of Strategic Services (OSS), as Marine Raiders, and as Paramarines. These experiences provided the foundation and forged the capabilities of today's Marine Forces Special Operations Command (MARFORSOC). The assessment and selection process used by the OSS identified those individuals that would be best suited to acquire a unique combination of individual skills and conduct dangerous missions where either success or failure would have strategic effects.

OFFICE OF STRATEGIC SERVICES

The OSS was formed to provide reliable intelligence from behind enemy lines. The OSS needed people who could speak local languages and maintain a calm sense of situational awareness in an environment fraught with spies, saboteurs, and collaborators. Fifty-one Marines would serve with distinction in these clandestine special operations missions.

Laura Lacey's *Ortiz: To Live a Man's Life* spotlights the remarkable story of one Marine who served in the OSS: Colonel Peter Julien Ortiz. Private Ortiz enlisted in the Marine Corps in June 1942. Based upon his previous military experience in the French Foreign Legion and performance at the Marine Corps Recruit Depot, he received a commission in August 1942. Being a native French speaker and possessing a working ability to speak German, Spanish, and Arabic, he was assigned to the Naval Command, OSS.

As Robert Mattingly described in *Herringbone Cloak—G.I. Dagger Marines of the OSS*, in 1944, Major Ortiz was placed in command of an operational group called Union II (see fig. 1-2). This was a heavily armed contingent that parachuted into the vicinity of Col des Saisies, France, to

Figure 1-2.The Union II team the day after the jump (2 August 1944) near Col des Saisies. From left to right: Sergeant John Bodnar, Major Peter Ortiz (code name Chambellan), Gunnery Sergeant Robert La Salle, Sergeant Fred Brunner, Captain Frank Coolidge (US Army Air Forces) (code name Aimant), and Sergeant Jack Risler. All except Captain Coolidge were Marines.

conduct direct action missions. Accompanying Major Ortiz on these missions was Gunnery Sergeant Robert La Salle and Sergeants Charles Perry, John P. Bodnar, Frederick J. Brunner, and Jack R. Risler—all Marines.

The accomplishments of the Union II team during World War II demonstrated the strategic effect of small teams comprised of screened and selected individuals. These teams blended the art of operations and intelligence against priority targets in support of the overall campaign. The methods and effects established during this period matured into the special operations capabilities employed today.

While the OSS Marines provided the foundation for strategic and special reconnaissance, the Marine Raiders conducted raids and other operations directly related to what is known today as direct action.

MARINE RAIDERS

During World War II, President Franklin Delano Roosevelt, supported by other influential political and military leaders within the United States, was determined to establish an organization of small teams that would bring the war to our enemies as rapidly as possible, utilizing the minimum amount of manpower while producing maximum effects. The Marine Corps was the ideal parent organization for this new commando-type unit because of the Marines' historical successes in small wars and the recent development of amphibious operational concepts. The Marine Corps initially opposed the establishment of special units or raiding parties, stating in Charles L. Updegraph's *Special Marine Corps Units of World War II* that the term "Marine" was alone sufficient "to indicate a man ready for duty at any time and that the injection of a special name, such as commando, would be undesirable and superfluous." Despite institutional opposition, in January 1942 the United States Marine Corps established two Raider battalions. The mission of the new Raider units was to be the spearhead of amphibious landings by larger forces thought to be inaccessible, to conduct raiding expeditions requiring great elements of speed and surprise, and to conduct guerilla-type operations for protracted periods behind enemy lines. The Raiders consisted of volunteers who were then screened and assessed to ensure their attributes were compatible with the type of anticipated mission. The Marine Raiders were required to be intellectually dynamic, morally disciplined, and physically fit operators with an irrepressible sense of duty, loyalty to one another, and in possession of a can-do-spirit in the face of adversity.

Typical of "commando" units at the time, the Raider volunteers received unique training and equipment. Initial equipment requests included such "exotic" items as riot shotguns, collapsible bicycles, chain saws, rubber boats, and sufficient automatic pistols to issue one per Raider.

The Marine Raiders conducted missions in the Pacific during World War II and added significant history to Marine Corps lineage. The Raider battalions' initial operations conducted in 1942 included the 1st Raider Battalion landing at Tulagi in support of the Guadalcanal landings, while the 2d Raider Battalion conducted a diversionary raid on Makin Island. The Raider battalions continued to conduct combat operations in the Pacific, participating in the landings at Guadalcanal, New Georgia, and Bougainville (see fig. 1-3).

In early 1944, the requirement for Raiders in the Pacific had changed; there was no longer the demand justifying the employment of special units. The Chief of Naval Operations approved the transfer and reflagging of the 1st and 2d Raider Battalions to the 4th Marine Regiment.

No longer having units specifically organized and tasked to conduct special operations, the Marine Corps continued the legacy of the "small wars" philosophy with reconnaissance units conducting long-range patrols and infantry units interacting with the local population through programs like the Combined Action Program in Vietnam. A few select Marines were also assigned to billets outside of the Marine Corps to conduct or directly support special operations.

Figure 1-3. Marine Raiders on Bougainville, January 1944.

VIETNAM

Marine Corps contributions to special operations during the Vietnam era were small in comparison to the other Services, but persistent throughout the conflict. Marines assigned to reconnaissance elements conducted Operations Keyhole (information gathering) and Stingray (direct action). Marine aviation elements provided direct support to the Military Assistance Command, Vietnam (Studies and Observations Group) missions. This group was a highly-classified, multi-Service special operations unit that conducted covert warfare operations.

Major James Capers, Jr., USMC, accomplished a wide variety of special operations tasks during his tours in the Republic of Vietnam while serving as a reconnaissance officer. He conducted long-range reconnaissance patrols, led a team of combat divers in Nha Trang Harbor searching for saboteurs and explosives, and participated in Operation Double Talk attempting to rescue prisoners of war behind enemy lines.

Lieutenant Colonel George "Digger" O'Dell served as a force reconnaissance officer in Vietnam from 1965 to 1968, at which point he left the Marine Corps to pursue a career as a Central Intelligence Agency paramilitary officer, serving in Laos and the Middle East from 1969 to 1975. Lieutenant Colonel O'Dell eventually returned to the Marine Corps, providing a wealth of knowledge on special operations. Based upon his knowledge and experience, he provided recommendations on how the Marine Corps would best participate in and support special operations. He formulated recommendations for the new Marine expeditionary unit (special operations capable) (MEU[SOC]) program through interagency information exchanges, and provided significant contributions to the Marine Corps' development of the initial close-quarters battle and explosive breaching programs. He served in multiple reconnaissance units and completed joint billets with the joint special operations command and the Naval Special Warfare Command over the course of his 27-year career. His contributions to the Marine Corps and the special operations community have been described as immeasurable.

COLD WAR ERA

The end of the Vietnam War saw a reduction in special operations units across all the Services due to force reductions. The global environment continued to change, allowing terrorism to take various forms and present asymmetric threats to the United States.

Post-Vietnam, the Marine Corps did not possess special operations units. The Marine Corps did retain its organic ground reconnaissance units that possessed similar capabilities at the tactical level in order to support Marine air-ground task force (MAGTF) operations with ground intelligence, surveillance, and reconnaissance requirements.

During this period, the Marine Corps continued to discreetly support the national defense strategy by providing selected individuals to special operations assignments. These individuals proved to be "quiet professionals" conducting special operations in the Middle East, Europe, and Latin America.

The United States conducted Operation Eagle Claw in April of 1980. The mission was to rescue 52 Americans held hostage in Iran. The task force was an ad hoc organization with elements provided from the different Services. The United States Marine Corps supported the operation with an aviation element. The mission failed, resulting in the death of eight Service members at a location known as "Desert One" in the Dasht-e-Kavir area of Iran.

The Joint Chiefs of Staff established a Special Operations Review Group, headed by retired Chief of Naval Operations, Admiral James L. Holloway III, to conduct an independent review of the rescue operation. The membership of the group represented the four Services; the Marine Corps participant was Major General Alfred M. Gray, Jr., who was selected for his ground combat leadership experience in Korea and Vietnam involving intelligence, reconnaissance, and special operations.

The Joint Chiefs of Staff commissioned the Special Operations Review Group in May of 1980. Based upon the 23 issues analyzed, it was recommended that a counterterrorist joint task force (JTF) be established with permanent assignment of staff and forces. Based upon the findings of the report, in 1986 the US Congress passed legislation known as the Cohen-Nunn Amendment to the Goldwater-Nichols Act to establish USSOCOM, which was activated on 16 April 1987.

As presented in Lieutenant Colonel Mark A. Clark's *USAWC Strategy Research Project: Should the Marine Corps Expand its Role in Special Operations?*, General Gray, as Commandant of the Marine Corps, announced on 5 February 1988 that the Marine Corps was changing the designations of the MAGTF, and the term "amphibious" was replaced by "expeditionary." These changes communicated that the Marine amphibious units, later renamed Marine expeditionary units (MEU), were capable of more than amphibious operations and could operate as a force of choice for the full range of military operations.

During the MEU predeployment training cycle, the MAGTF would conduct a certification to be identified as special operations capable. The MEU(SOC) would then forward deploy from their parent Marine expeditionary force and conduct regional operations with the capability to perform or enable crisis response, limited contingency operations, and enable the introduction of follow-on forces and designated special operations. The MEU(SOC)'s signature attribute was the ability to rapidly plan, coordinate, and execute operations, to include the conduct of limited special operations when directed.

MARINE CORPS UNITED STATES SPECIAL OPERATIONS COMMAND DETACHMENT

Just as the complex global environment preceding US involvement in World War II prompted the development of the Marine Raiders, the complex global environment of the global war on terrorism prompted the need for an additional capacity of small teams capable of achieving operational and strategic effects. The attack on the World Trade Center on 11 September 2001 stretched the Nation's special operations forces (SOF) extremely thin and Secretary of Defense Donald Rumsfeld called for the Marines to be part of USSOCOM. The Marine Corps United States Special Operations Command Detachment (MCSOCOM DET) was activated on 20 June 2003 and deployed to Iraq for Operation Iraqi Freedom in March 2004 (see fig. 1-4). The MCSOCOM DET proved to the other special operations components that the Marine Corps could perform special operations missions such as direct action, special reconnaissance, foreign internal defense (FID), counterterrorism, and other special activities. The MCSOCOM DET was deactivated on 10 March 2006, but the successful employment of the MCSOCOM DET laid the groundwork for the formation of United States Marine Corps Forces, Special Operations Command (MARSOC).

In his after-action review to the commander of Naval Special Warfare Command, the MCSOCOM DET Commander, Colonel Robert J. Coates, stressed the value of the detachment's task organization by emphasizing that the detachment brought capabilities to USSOCOM that it did not otherwise possess in a standalone unit. The detachment could perform all six warfighting

Figure 1-4. Marine Corps United States Special Operations Command Detachment Operation Iraqi Freedom 2004.

functions: command and control (C2), fires, maneuver, logistics, intelligence, and force protection. The detachment also had the ability to provide effective depth-to-field liaison officers to various commands and agencies, and it could operate either as a supporting effort or a main effort with equal facility.

UNITED STATES MARINE CORPS FORCES, SPECIAL OPERATIONS COMMAND

On 23 November 2005, the Secretary of Defense announced the creation of MARSOC. The MARSOC was assigned the mission to recruit, organize, train, equip, and deploy task-organized, scalable, expeditionary Marine Corps SOF worldwide to accomplish the full spectrum of special operations missions assigned by the Commander, United States Special Operations Command (CDRUSSOCOM), the geographic combatant commanders (GCCs) via the theater special operations command (TSOC), or both.

On 24 February 2006, MARSOC was designated a special operations forces Service component to USSOCOM and activated at Camp Lejeune, North Carolina. Initially, MARSOC was formed from a small staff from the 4th Marine Expeditionary Brigade and the Foreign Military Training Unit (commonly referred to as FMTU) that had been formed to conduct FID. In the months following the activation, MARSOC rounded out its operating forces with the transfer of structure and personnel from 1st and 2d Force Reconnaissance Companies. These companies would form the nucleus of 1st and 2d Marine Special Operations Battalions. The Foreign Military Training Unit was later redesignated as the Marine Special Operations Advisory Group and, subsequently, 3d Marine Special Operations Battalion. Elements of the Marine Special Operations Advisory Group also provided a significant portion of the manpower required to staff the new Marine Special Operations Regiment, which was activated in 2009. Six months after its activation, MARSOC deployed its first operational teams in support of USSOCOM and the geographic combatant commands. The first company-sized deployments began in 2007 in support of Operation Enduring Freedom.

In 2015, Headquarters, United States Marine Corps (HQMC) authorized MARFORSOC to redesignate subordinate units as "Marine Raiders." This action was authorized to reflect upon the linkage to the Marine Raiders of World War II. This same year *Spiritus Invictus* was officially designated as the MARFORSOC motto reflecting an unconquerable spirit.

SHAPING THE FORCE

The nature of special operations demands that MARFORSOC develop Marines to operate across the range of military operations. This is accomplished by organizing and equipping Marines to succeed in demanding environments, often with limited external support. The MARFORSOC continues to develop and refine skills and equipment to operate as an independent SOF element, forward deployed with the capability to command and control distributed teams. This concept best supports the GCC and conventional forces through all the joint operational phases. Marine Forces Special Operations Command will continue to focus on regionalization while maintaining the flexibility to surge and rapidly deploy in response to a crisis. In order to posture the force for employment, MARFORSOC must develop projection capabilities from land- and sea-based platforms to provide SOF capabilities that produce strategic effects. The key strengths of Marine special operations forces (MARSOF) are the combination of organizational agility, adaptability, and expeditionary nature that enable timely deployment in interest of national security.

Marine Forces Special Operations Command is organized into a headquarters element, a Marine Special Operations School (MSOS), a Marine Raider Support Group, and a Marine Raider Regiment. Marines, Sailors, and civilians assigned to MARFORSOC have continuously deployed to Central, Pacific, Africa, and Southern Commands areas of responsibility (AORs).

The MARFORSOC conducts tactical operations to achieve operational- or strategic-level effects. Marine special operations forces are specially selected and trained Marines that conduct SOF core activities to include direct action, special reconnaissance, security force assistance (SFA), counterterrorism, FID, and COIN, while supporting countering weapons of mass destruction (CWMD) and unconventional warfare in hostile, denied, and politically sensitive environments.

The foundation of MARFORSOC is people. Marine Corps special operations foundational principles, concepts, legacies, and values are represented within the MARFORSOC ethos. Organizationally, MARFORSOC collectively builds upon the Marine Corps ethos of—

- Marines dedicated and imbued with the idea of selfless service to our Nation.
- A force, expeditionary in nature, deploying anywhere in the world with responsive, scalable, and adaptable forces prepared to "live hard" in uncertain, chaotic, and austere environments, yet capable of sustainable expeditionary operations.
- Units forged and task-organized to be lean, agile, and adaptable.
- Units trained and equipped to lead joint and multinational operations and enable interagency activities.
- Marines educated and trained to think critically about complex environments and empowered with the judgment and initiative to defeat our adversaries regardless of the conflict.
- A command structure committed to the resilience of our Marines and their families.

The MARFORSOC selects Marines based on very specific attributes (the "right" Marine versus the "best" Marine) and builds upon their foundation of Marine Corps values and warrior ethos by imbuing in them a mentality of *Spiritus Invictus*—an unconquerable spirit. Marine Forces Special

Operations Command then provides the right Marine with unique SOF training and equipment and instills a holistic—body, mind, and spirit—approach to resiliency. The MARFORSOC ethos enables the deployment of small, lethal, expeditionary teams capable of executing complex distributed operations to achieve strategic and operational effects.

The MARFORSOC's traditional Corps values and warrior ethos embraces and complements five SOF truths, which are—

- Humans are more important than hardware.
- Quality is better than quantity.
- SOF cannot be mass-produced.
- Competent SOF cannot be created after emergencies occur.
- Most special operations require non-SOF support.

The five SOF truths are time-proven and vital considerations for the development and sustainment of any special operations capability.

This Page Intentionally Left Blank

CHAPTER 2
SPECIAL OPERATIONS FUNDAMENTALS

Marine SOF conduct the full range of assigned special operations in any environment, with a focus on sustainable expeditionary special operations in support of the combatant commanders. Marine SOF's conduct of special operations is unique amongst SOF components, as these operations are executed by a reinforced company consisting of multidiscipline intelligence, communications, logistics, joint terminal attack controller (JTAC), multi-purpose canine (MPC), and explosive ordnance disposal (EOD) support, as well as other organic combat service support (CSS).

Special operations are conducted in hostile, denied, or politically sensitive environments to achieve diplomatic, informational, military, and/or economic objectives by employing military capabilities for which there is no broad, conventional force requirement. These operations may require low visibility, unique skills, and/or clandestine capabilities. Special operations are applicable across the range of military operations. They can be conducted independently or in conjunction with operations of conventional forces or other government agencies, and they may include operations by and with indigenous or surrogate forces. Special operations differ from conventional operations in the degree of physical and political risk, operational techniques, mode of employment, independence from friendly support, and dependence on detailed operational intelligence and indigenous assets.

Special operations forces are specially selected, organized, trained, and equipped military forces characterized by individual and small-unit proficiency, specialized skills, small size, low visibility, clandestine methodologies, and the ability to operate in austere environments, often with minimal logistic support. As such, SOF may provide commanders a reduced signature and scalable response option that reduces the political risk that typically accompanies the employment of a larger, more visible conventional force. However, commanders must ensure that the expected outcome of a mission is commensurate with the associated risk, balancing the limited resources of SOF against the operational advantages of special operations.

Special operations differ from conventional operations by the nature of the capability required to accomplish the mission, the environment in which the mission is being conducted, the attendant risk or political sensitivity associated with the mission, or a combination of all three factors. Hence, a mission that might typically be conducted by conventional forces may, under certain operational parameters, require the application of special operations skills and techniques. For example, a FID mission to train indigenous conventional forces in infantry tactics might require the low visibility of SOF depending on the threat environment and the political sensitivity associated with having a foreign military operating within a region.

CHARACTERISTICS OF SPECIAL OPERATIONS

The following list is by no means comprehensive; rather it is intended to highlight those aspects of special operations and SOF that combine to make them unique in comparison to conventional military operations:

- SOF is typically task-organized to provide a tailored military response to specific situations or crises requiring precise effects.
- SOF can operate independently or as a supporting or supported force with conventional forces. Regardless, special operations execution is typically decentralized and places a premium on individual initiative.
- Special operations are inherently joint. Even in instances where a single Service is conducting special operations, joint support and coordination is required. In many instances, interagency support and coordination may also be required.
- SOF is best employed when the use of conventional forces is inappropriate or unfeasible. As with all specialized troops, SOF should not be used as a substitute for other forces.
- Special operations typically employ deception, stealth, surprise, tempo, and other measures to achieve success and counterbalance the small footprint and limited firepower typical of SOF.
- Special operations typically require advanced communications, infiltration and exfiltration techniques, and support given the nature of the operating environment in politically sensitive and/or hostile areas.
- Special operations frequently involve cooperation with indigenous and irregular forces that require a high degree of operational patience and long-term commitment to achieve operational/strategic goals.
- Special operations involving indigenous and irregular forces require detailed knowledge of the local cultures, languages, and areas of operations demanding specially selected and trained personnel with a high level of competence, maturity, and regional expertise.
- Special operations frequently require a discriminate and precise application of force, often employing a mix of high- and low-technology weapons and equipment not resident in conventional military forces.

SPECIAL OPERATIONS FORCES MISSION CRITERIA

Six basic criteria assist SOF and non-SOF commanders and planners in determining whether a mission is an appropriate use of SOF. While some of the criteria are common sense and apply equally to conventional as well as special operations, others are peculiar to SOF. Special operations forces mission criteria are as follows:

- The mission or task must be appropriate for SOF. The desired effects must be outside the scope of conventional forces and require the application of SOF-peculiar skills and capabilities.
- The mission or task should support the higher campaign or operation plan. A mission or task is invalid if it does not support achieving the end state of a higher campaign or operation.
- The mission or task must be operationally feasible, fully approved, and coordinated.
- The mission's objective must fall within the capability of the tasked SOF unit to perform.
- The resources required to execute the SOF mission must be available. As stated in the fifth SOF truth, special operations missions generally require non-SOF support to succeed. This is especially true for long-term operations and operations involving host nation (HN) forces whose own supporting assets are limited. Lack of required support (e.g., assault support, intelligence, communications support) may render an otherwise viable special operations mission unfeasible.
- The expected outcome of the mission must justify the risks. As with all assets that are high value but limited in numbers, supported commanders must ensure that expected benefits of conducting the mission are commensurate with its inherent risks. Once depleted, the specialized capability of SOF cannot be quickly replaced.

PREPARATION OF THE ENVIRONMENT

Special operations forces take actions to prepare the operational environment for potential operations. Preparation of the environment (PE) is conducted during the shaping phase of an operation, as well as for developing and preparing for the entry of forces, and supporting agencies to resolve conflicts using either lethal or nonlethal action. Preparation of the environment supports special operations advance force operations (AFO) being conducted to refine the location of specific, identified targets and further develop the operational environment. Special operations AFO encompasses many PE activities, but are intended to prepare for near-term direct action. Special operations AFO may include, but are not limited to, close target reconnaissance; tagging, tracking, and locating; reception, staging, onward movement, and integration of forces; infrastructure development; and terminal guidance. Unless specifically withheld, special operations AFO also includes direct action in situations when failure to act will mean loss of a fleeting opportunity for success.

SPECIAL OPERATIONS FORCES CORE ACTIVITIES

Understanding the core activities assigned to USSOCOM is critical to understanding how MARFORSOC is organized, trained, equipped, and employed. The USSOCOM performs tasks no other forces in the Department of Defense (DOD) conduct. The USSOCOM also performs tasks conducted by conventional forces. However, these tasks are associated with a unique set of conditions and standards using tactics, techniques, and procedures (TTP) and equipment that conventional forces do not possess.

Special operations forces core activities are operationally significant and unique capabilities applied in different combinations tailored toward the operational requirement. The core activities can be applied independently or in combination as part of global, GCC, or joint force commander (JFC) campaign, operation, or activity.

The USSOCOM core activities (Joint Publication [JP] 3-05, *Special Operations*) are as follows:

- Direct action.
- Special reconnaissance.
- CWMD.
- Counterterrorism.
- Unconventional warfare.
- FID.
- SFA.
- Hostage rescue and recovery.
- COIN.
- Foreign humanitarian assistance.
- Military information support operations (MISO).
- Civil affairs operations (CAO).

Commander, United States Special Operations Command has assigned Commander, Marine Forces Special Operations Command (COMMARFORSOC) the following SOF core activities:

- Direct action.
- Special reconnaissance.
- Counterterrorism.
- FID.
- SFA.
- COIN.
- Support to CWMD.
- Support to unconventional warfare.

Although not assigned specifically, MARFORSOC will support the other SOF core activities of hostage rescue and recovery, foreign humanitarian assistance, MISO, and CAO, as required.

DIRECT ACTION

Direct action refers to short-duration strikes and other small-scale offensive actions conducted as a special operation in hostile, denied, or diplomatically-sensitive environments, and employing specialized military capabilities to seize, destroy, capture, exploit, recover, or damage designated targets. Direct action differs from conventional offensive actions in the level of physical and political risk, operational techniques, and the degree of discriminate and precise use of force to achieve specific objectives. The MARFORSOC conducts direct action as a core activity. In the conduct of these operations, SOF may employ raid, ambush, or direct assault tactics (including close-quarters battle); emplace mines and other munitions; conduct standoff attacks by fire from air, ground, or maritime platforms; provide terminal guidance for precision-guided munitions; conduct independent sabotage; and conduct antiship operations.

Special operations forces may conduct direct action operations independently or as part of larger conventional or unconventional operations or campaigns. Although normally considered close combat-type operations, direct action operations also include sniping and other standoff attacks by fire delivered or directed by SOF. Standoff attacks are preferred when the target can be damaged or destroyed without close combat. Special operations forces employ close combat tactics and techniques when the mission requires the precise or discriminate use of force or the recovery or capture of personnel or materiel.

Direct action missions may also involve locating, recovering, and restoring to friendly control selected persons or materiel that are isolated and threatened in sensitive, denied, or contested areas. These missions usually result from situations that involve political sensitivity or military criticality of the personnel or materiel being recovered from remote or hostile environments. These situations may arise from a political change, combat action, chance happening, or mechanical mishap. Direct action operations differ from combat search and rescue by the use of dedicated ground combat elements, unconventional techniques, precise survivor intelligence, or indigenous assistance.

Direct action operations may be unilateral or combined actions but are still precise, of short duration, and discrete in nature. A SOF chain of command executes direct action operations to achieve the supported commander's objectives. Unlike unconventional warfare operations, direct action operations do not necessarily involve or require the support of an indigenous or surrogate chain of command to achieve objectives of mutual interest.

SPECIAL RECONNAISSANCE

Special reconnaissance is defined as reconnaissance and surveillance actions conducted as a special operation in hostile, denied, or politically-sensitive environments to collect or verify information of strategic or operational significance, employing military capabilities not normally found in conventional forces. These actions provide an additive capability for commanders and supplement other reconnaissance and surveillance actions. Marine Forces Special Operations Command conducts special reconnaissance as a core activity.

Special reconnaissance may include gathering information on activities of an actual or potential enemy or securing data on the meteorological, hydrographic, or geographic characteristics of a particular area. Special reconnaissance may also include assessment of chemical, biological, residual nuclear, or environmental hazards in a denied area. Special reconnaissance includes target acquisition, area assessment, and post-strike reconnaissance.

Special reconnaissance complements national and theater operations and intelligence collection assets and systems by obtaining specific, well-defined, and time-sensitive information of strategic or operational significance. Special reconnaissance may complement other collection methods constrained by weather, terrain-masking, or hostile countermeasures. When authorized, selected SOF conduct special reconnaissance as a human intelligence activity placing US or US-controlled personnel, or "eyes on target," in hostile, denied, or politically sensitive territory.

In the operational environment, the SOF and conventional command relationship may be supported or supporting, rather than tactical control or operational control (OPCON). Using SOF with conventional forces by a JFC creates an additional and unique capability to achieve objectives that may not be otherwise attainable. Using SOF for special reconnaissance enables the JFC to maximize unity of effort and take advantage of SOF core competencies to enhance situational awareness and facilitate staff planning of and training for integrated operations. Special operations forces should not be used as dedicated reconnaissance assets for conventional forces. Instead, the JFC, through a joint special operations task force (JSOTF) or a TSOC, may task a SOF element to provide special reconnaissance information to conventional forces that may be operating for a period of time within a joint special operations area, or may task a SOF element on a case-by-case basis to conduct special reconnaissance within a conventional forces AOR. Special operations forces and conventional elements working within the same AOR may develop formal or informal information sharing relationships that enhance each other's operational capabilities and emphasize unity of purpose in pursuit of achieving a shared end state.

COUNTERTERRORISM

Counterterrorism is defined as "activities and operations taken to neutralize terrorists and their organizations and networks in order to render them incapable of using violence to instill fear and coerce governments or societies to achieve their goals". (JP 3-26, *Counterterrorism*) Special operations forces possess the capability to conduct these operations in environments that may be denied to conventional forces because of political or threat conditions. Marine Forces Special Operations Command conducts counterterrorism as a primary core activity.

In addition to being a SOF core activity, counterterrorism is part of the DOD's broader construct of combating terrorism, which is "actions, including antiterrorism and counterterrorism, taken to oppose terrorism throughout the entire threat spectrum". (JP 3-26) Success in the global counterterrorism effort requires interorganizational coordination to maximize the effectiveness of all the instruments of national power of the United States and partner nations. As the integrating command for global counterterrorism planning efforts, USSOCOM supports a global combating terrorism network (GCTN)—a growing network of relationships and liaison partnerships, a supporting technical infrastructure, and the use of information sharing policies. Along with US interagency partners, this network draws upon an increasing number of countries, regional organizations, intergovernmental organizations, nongovernmental organizations, and the private sector to achieve unified action.

The DOD global campaign plan for the war on terrorism requires integration of direct and indirect approaches:

- *Direct Approach.* The direct approach consists of actions taken against terrorists and terrorist organizations. The goals of the direct approach against terrorists and their organizations are to defeat a specific threat through neutralization or dismantlement of the network (including actors, resources, and support structures) and to prevent the re-emergence of a threat, once neutralized. Using the direct approach, several SOF core activities may be required to accomplish the following tasks against terrorist organizations:
  - *Intelligence Operations.* These operations collect, exploit, and report information on the functions and resources terrorist organizations require. Special operations forces have the capability to conduct these operations in an overt or clandestine manner.
  - *Network and Infrastructure Attacks.* These operations involve preemptive strikes against terrorist organizations with the objective of destroying, disorganizing, or disarming terrorist organizations before they can strike targets of national interest.
  - *Hostage or Sensitive Materiel Recovery.* These operations rescue hostages and/or recover sensitive material from terrorist control, requiring capabilities not normally found in conventional military units. The safety of the hostages and prevented destruction of the sensitive materiel are essential mission requirements.
- *Indirect Approach.* The indirect approach consists of the means by which the GCTN can influence the operational environments within which counterterrorism operations/campaigns are conducted. This approach usually includes actions taken to enable GCTN partners to conduct operations against terrorists and their organizations, to shape and stabilize the operational environments in order to erode the capabilities of terrorist organizations, and to degrade the terrorist's ability to acquire support and sanctuary. The indirect approach includes use of the SOF core activities such as unconventional warfare, FID, SFA, CAO, and MISO.

The ability to manage both approaches and harness their synergistic effects is vital to the success of near- and long-term counterterrorism objectives, whether within the scope of a theater operation/campaign or the global campaign.

FOREIGN INTERNAL DEFENSE

Foreign internal defense is the participation by civilian and military agencies of a government in any of the action programs taken by another government or other designated organization to free and protect its society from subversion, lawlessness, and insurgency. Marine Forces Special Operations Command conducts FID as a core activity.

Foreign internal defense is an umbrella concept covering a broad range of activities and may involve all instruments of national power. Its primary intent is to help the legitimate host government address internal threats and their underlying causes. Commensurate with US policy goals, the focus of all US

FID efforts is to support the United States Government's (USG's) program of internal defense and development (IDAD) for that particular country. The entire FID effort is tailored to the needs of the individual nation and designed to support the HN IDAD strategy.

United States Special Operations Command is the only combatant command with FID as a legislatively mandated core task. In fulfilling this core task, USSOCOM provides SOF in support of GCCs. In addition to dedicated theater forces, SOF units typically contribute to the FID effort under the OPCON of the TSOC, which has primary responsibility to plan and supervise the execution of SOF operations in support of FID. However, FID operations other than combat may have a direct coordination relationship with the chief of mission or the designee at the US Embassy.

Special operations forces may conduct FID operations unilaterally in the absence of any other military effort, support other ongoing military or civilian assistance efforts, or support the employment of conventional forces. In smaller FID operations, SOF units may compose the majority of the force or may entirely make up the force. The opposite may be true as well; in a large FID operation, caps on total troop numbers may result in a disproportionally smaller number of SOF personnel than conventional forces. Once FID operations are initiated, programs may be handed over to conventional forces. In addition, extended long-term programs may be handed off to conventional forces at some point. In both cases, SOF units may still have a prominent supporting role, although their focus may shift to training HN SOF.

Foreign internal defense also supports stability operations. These operations promote and protect US national interests by influencing the threat, political, and information operational variables through a combination of peacetime developmental, cooperative activities, and coercive actions in response to crises. Special operations forces accomplish stability goals through security cooperation. The military activities that support these operations are diverse, continuous, and often long-term. Their purpose is to promote and sustain regional and global stability. Stability operations employ forces, including SOF and civil affairs, to assist civil authorities, foreign or domestic, as they prepare for or respond to crises. The primary role of stability operations is to meet the immediate needs of designated groups for a limited time, until civil authorities can accomplish these tasks without military assistance.

Foreign internal defense is not restricted to times of conflict; it can also take place in the form of training exercises and other activities that show the US resolve to and for the region. These exercises train the host nation to deal with potential internal threats. Foreign internal defense usually consists of indirect assistance, such as participation in combined exercises and training programs or limited direct assistance without US participation in combat operations. These actions support the host nation in establishing IDAD programs.

Special operations forces primary roles in FID are to assess, train, advise, assist, and support HN military and paramilitary forces with tasks that require the unique capabilities of SOF, conduct CAO to enhance the relationship between military forces and civil authorities in areas where military forces are present, and conduct MISO to promote the ability of the host nation to defeat internally- and externally-based insurgencies and terrorism by encouraging the population to actively support the HN military and government, while restricting the enemy's movement and denying access to the local population. As previously mentioned, SOF may also conduct specialized missions in support of combat operations. The goal is to enable these forces to maintain the host nation's internal stability, to counter subversion and violence in their country, and to address the causes of instability. Each of these key SOF FID activities plays a role in the accomplishment of the HN IDAD strategy—

- *HN Military Assistance.* Operations that train HN military individuals and units in tactical employment, sustainment, and integration of land, air, and maritime skills; provide advice and assistance to military leaders; provide training on TTP required to protect the host nation from subversion, lawlessness, and insurgency; and develop indigenous individual, leader, and organizational skills.
- *Population Security.* Operations that strengthen population security by providing supervision of tactical operations conducted by HN military units to neutralize and destroy insurgent threats, isolate insurgents from the civil population, and protect the civil population. As a subset of FID, designated SOF units may also train select HN forces to perform counterterrorist missions.
- *Counterinsurgency.* Counterinsurgency is the "comprehensive civilian and military efforts designed to simultaneously defeat and contain insurgency and address its root causes." (JP 1-02) These operations promote a safe and secure environment within which government institutions can address the concerns of the people and separate the population from the insurgents. Military operations that may be in support of COIN fall into the following three broad categories:
  - *Civil-Military Operations.* These activities establish, maintain, influence, or exploit relations between military forces, indigenous populations, and institutions by directly supporting the attainment of objectives relating to the re-establishment or maintenance of stability within a region or host nation. These activities may occur prior to, during, or subsequent to other military actions. They may also occur, if directed, in the absence of other military operations. Civil-military operations may be performed by designated civil affairs, by other military forces, or by a combination of civil affairs and other forces.
  - *Combat Operations.* Combat operations are oriented against insurgent leaders and cadre, smaller units, and insurgent main force organizations (battalions, brigades, division-sized units), depending on the phase of the insurgency. Although the USG does not normally commit its forces to combat against foreign insurgents, SOF may accompany HN forces on tactical COIN operations, particularly in the early stages of COIN, to instill confidence in the HN forces. However, COIN is the host nation's responsibility and HN forces must be responsible for their own combat operations.
  - *Information Operations.* The information operations objective is to execute, as a secondary core MARFORSOC mission, those capabilities that enable our forces to influence and shape the environment to their advantage while in a supported command's AOR. Information operations consists of all of the information means and techniques available for employment during military operations to leverage any or all information-related capabilities in concert with other lines of operations to influence, disrupt, corrupt, deny, isolate, destroy, or usurp the decision-making or information advantage of adversaries, insurgents, extremists, or potential adversaries, along with their supporting elements, while protecting our own and partner nation forces.

Foreign internal defense operations are planned at the national, regional, and, especially with SOF units, at the local level. The FID effort should involve the integration of all instruments of national power down to the local level. Ideally, the HN's IDAD goals can be met by skillful use of diplomatic, informational, and economic instruments without the military instrument; however, historically this has not been the case. Foreign internal defense operations fall under two major categories—those under the responsibility of the DOD and those under the responsibility of the Department of State (DOS). Foreign internal defense has certain aspects that make planning complex. Some basic imperatives when integrating FID into strategies and plans are—

- *Understanding US Foreign Policy.* National level directives, plans, or policies are the guiding documents for understanding US foreign policy. Joint Strategic Planning System documents reflect the military's responsibilities for carrying out this broad guidance. Planners must be prepared to adjust FID plans as political conditions change in the host nation and the United States.
- *Maintaining and Increasing HN Sovereignty and Legitimacy.* If US military efforts in support of FID undermine the sovereignty or legitimacy of the HN government, then they have effectively sabotaged the IDAD program.
- *Understanding US Assistance Efforts Before Implementing FID Programs.* There are long-term and/or strategic implications and sustainability concerns for all US assistance efforts that are implemented in FID programs. Host nation development and defense self-sufficiency, both of which may require large investments of time and materiel, are especially important in planning for FID. The SOF FID planners assess the following:
  - The end state of the IDAD strategy (or country plan in lieu of a developed IDAD strategy).
  - The sustainability of development programs and defense improvements.
  - The acceptability and the perceptions of fairness of development models across the range of a HN society.
  - The impact of development programs on the distribution of resources within the host nation, to include potential shortages and bottlenecks.
  - The potential negative side effects of socioeconomic change.
  - The potential resistors to socioeconomic change.
  - The relationship between improved military forces and existing regional, ethnic, and religious groups in the military and society as a whole.
  - The impact of the improved military forces on the regional balance of power in the host nation.
  - The impact of military development and operations on civil-military relations in the host nation.
- *Tailoring Military Support of FID Programs to the Operational Environment and Specific HN Needs.* The threat, as well as the local religious, social, economic, and political factors, should be considered when developing military plans to support FID. Failure to consider these factors can result in equipment, training, and infrastructures that are either unsuitable and/or unsustainable by the host nation.

Foreign internal defense is a national-level effort that involves numerous USG agencies. In all cases, the DOS will play a significant role in providing the content of FID plans. In most cases, the DOS' role in planning will be significant because the chief of mission is typically the final approval authority for the FID plan in all situations not involving combat operations; the chief of mission remains a significant partner when FID planning involves combat operations. To reduce inefficiencies, contradictions, or redundancies in FID programs, all parties involved, both governmental and nongovernmental, must be coordinated to ensure an integrated theater effort.

SECURITY FORCE ASSISTANCE

Security force assistance is any DOD activity that contributes to unified action by the USG to support the development of the capacity and capability of foreign security forces (FSF) and their supporting institutions. Security force assistance refers to all efforts designed to assess, generate, employ, sustain, and assist existing HN or regional security forces. Foreign internal defense may include SFA to build HN capacity in order to anticipate, preclude, and counter threats or potential threats, particularly when the host nation has not attained self-sufficiency and is faced with military threats beyond its capability. This helps the host nation address the root causes of instability in a preventive manner rather than reacting to threats. Marine Special Forces Operations Command conducts SFA as a core activity.

Security force assistance includes *organizing*, *training*, *equipping*, *rebuilding*, and *advising* various components of security forces; however, SOF performing SFA has to initially assess the FSF they will assist and then establish a shared, continued method of assessment throughout development of the FSF:

- *Organizing*. Organizing includes shaping institutions and units, which can range from standing up a ministry to improving the organization of the smallest maneuver unit. Building capability and capacity in this area includes personnel, logistics, and intelligence and their support infrastructure. Developing HN tactical capabilities alone is inadequate; strategic and operational capabilities must be developed as well. Host nation organizations and units should reflect their own unique requirements, interests, and capabilities—they should not simply mirror existing external institutions.
- *Training*. Training occurs in training centers, academies, and within units. Training includes a broad range of subject matter, to include security forces responding to civilian oversight and control.
- *Equipping*. Equipping is accomplished through traditional security assistance, foreign support, and donations. The equipment must be suitable for the physical environment of the region and the host nation's ability to sustain and operate it.
- *Rebuilding*. Rebuilding infrastructure after major combat operations may be necessary to support FSF. Infrastructure can include facilities for life support, command and control, as well as transportation and logistic networks.
- *Advising*. Advising HN units and institutions is essential to the ultimate success of SFA. Advising benefits the host nation and the supporting external organizations. Advising requires specially trained SOF personnel who—
  - Understand the operational and cultural environment.
  - Provide effective leadership.
  - Build legitimacy.
  - Manage information.
  - Ensure unity of effort/unity of purpose.
  - Can sustain the advising tasks.

Conducting successful SFA operations require a specific mindset; a mindset that first and foremost focuses on working through or with FSF in order to support the HN's IDAD or regional organization's charter. Special operations forces conducting SFA need to understand that all actions must develop and demonstrate the legitimacy of the HN government at all levels.

COUNTERINSURGENCY

Counterinsurgency is the comprehensive civilian and military efforts designed to simultaneously defeat and contain insurgency and address its root causes. Insurgency will be a large and growing element of the security challenges in the 21st century. Special operations forces are a principal US military contribution to COIN. Special operations forces can provide light, agile, highly-capable teams that lend themselves to distributed operations working discretely among local communities. Special operations forces can also conduct complex counterterrorist operations. Marine Special Forces Operations Command conducts COIN as a core activity and, in conjunction with US Army Special Operations Command, is the USSOCOM coordinating component for COIN.

Special Operations Forces and Counterinsurgency Approaches

Special operations forces are essential to successful COIN operations. Their capacity to conduct a wide array of missions with HN security forces or to integrate with US conventional forces makes them particularly suitable for COIN operations. Special operations forces are adept at using an indirect approach to positively influence segments of the indigenous population. In a more balanced or direct approach to COIN, however, they should be used to complement rather than replace the role of conventional forces.

Special Operations Forces Core Activities and Counterinsurgency

Marine Forces Special Operations Command is organized, trained, and equipped to accomplish core activities that may be involved in COIN. Any of these special operations core activities may be conducted as part of a COIN operation. Marine Forces Special Operations Command must adhere to the same tenets of COIN as its conventional partners. Even if focused on direct action missions, SOF must be cognizant of the need to win and maintain popular support. Direct action missions may be required to kill or capture vital insurgent targets. Specific types of direct action are raids, ambushes, and direct assaults and standoff attacks. Marine Forces Special Operations Command may conduct special reconnaissance into insurgent strongholds or sanctuaries; these activities include environmental reconnaissance, armed reconnaissance, target and threat assessment, and post-strike reconnaissance. Terrorism is typically a part of any insurgency, the greatest concern that would affect a protracted insurgency is transnational terrorism taking advantage of the uncertain environment to impose its own purposes. Marine Forces Special Operations Command is capable of supporting HN counterterrorism efforts as part of the COIN operations. Marine Forces Special Operations Command can produce the best effects in the region by understanding the enemy and applying the SOF core activities in a balanced approach throughout the operational phases.

SUPPORT TO COUNTERING WEAPONS OF MASS DESTRUCTION

Countering weapons of mass destruction refers to nonproliferation, counterproliferation, and weapons of mass destruction consequence management. Weapons of mass destruction are chemical, biological, radiological, or nuclear weapons capable of a high order of destruction or causing mass casualties. Countering weapons of mass destruction excludes the means of transporting or propelling the weapons where such means is a separable and divisible part from the weapons. Special operations forces primarily have a role in nonproliferation and counterproliferation by providing expertise, materiel, and teams to support combatant commanders locating, tagging, and tracking weapons of mass destruction; conducting interdiction and other offensive operations in limited areas as required; building partnership capacity for conducting counterproliferation activities; conducting MISO to dissuade adversary reliance on weapons of mass destruction; and other specialized technical capabilities. United States Special Operations Command is responsible for synchronizing the planning of DOD efforts in support of other combatant commands, departmental priorities, and, as directed, other USG agencies in support of the DOD CWMD strategy.

SUPPORT TO UNCONVENTIONAL WARFARE

Unconventional warfare encompasses the activities conducted that enable a resistance movement or insurgency to coerce, disrupt, or overthrow a government or occupying power by operating through or with an underground, auxiliary, and guerrilla force in a denied area. The United States may engage in unconventional warfare as part of a major theater war or limited regional contingency, or in support of a resistance movement or an insurgency. Marine Forces Special Operations Command supports combatant commands, joint forces commands, and SOF headquarters conducting unconventional warfare.

The costs versus benefits of using unconventional warfare must be carefully considered before employment. Properly integrated and synchronized unconventional warfare operations can extend the application of military power for strategic goals. Unconventional warfare complements operations by giving the United States opportunities to seize the initiative through preemptive or clandestine offensive action.

The purpose of unconventional warfare is to support a resistance movement or insurgency, which may support conventional military operations. Political control and legitimacy of regimes are the issues. Therefore, unconventional warfare has strategic utility that can alter the balance of power between sovereign states. Such high stakes carry significant political risk in both the international and domestic political arenas and require sensitive execution. The necessity to operate with clandestine and covert means, with sometimes a varying mix of clandestine and covert ways, produces excellent intelligence within the unconventional warfare operating area (UWOA). As in all conflict scenarios short of large-scale, state-to-state warfare, the DOS, intelligence providers, and military forces must closely coordinate their activities to enable and safeguard sensitive unconventional warfare operations. A JFC typically tasks SOF to lead an unconventional warfare operation. It will usually require some interagency support and possibly some support by conventional forces. The prevailing strategic environment suggests a JFC and staff must be able to effectively conduct/support unconventional warfare operations simultaneously during both traditional warfare and irregular warfare. In other cases, SOF conducting irregular warfare (possibly including unconventional warfare operations) will be the main effort with conventional forces playing a much smaller and supporting role.

United States-sponsored unconventional warfare efforts generally pass through seven distinct phases—

- *Phase I: Preparation.* The preparation phase for unconventional warfare is part of a three-step process that consists of intelligence preparation of the operational environment, war planning, and shaping activities.
- *Phase II: Initial Contact.* Ideally, a pilot team should make initial contact with an established or potential irregular element.
- *Phase III: Infiltration.* During this phase, the SOF units infiltrate the UWOA to link up with the pilot team and/or irregular force.
- *Phase IV: Organization.* During the organization phase, the SOF unit begins to develop the capability of the irregular force. Depending on the size and scope of the effort, the size of this force can range from one individual to a resistance element of potentially any size.
- *Phase V: Buildup.* The buildup phase involves the expanding of the irregular elements and their capabilities to meet mission objectives. Special operations forces unit tasks include infiltration or procurement of equipment and supplies to support this expansion and subsequent operations.
- *Phase VI: Employment.* During the employment phase, indigenous or other irregular forces increasingly operate in a combat or hostile environment. These operations build in scope and size and range from interdiction with guerilla forces through combat to active intelligence collection with an indigenous informant network. Regardless of the type of operation, the overall purpose is to achieve strategic political military objectives.
- *Phase VII: Transition.* Transition is the final, most difficult, and most sensitive phase of unconventional warfare operations. The planning for transition begins when the USG decides to sponsor an irregular organization and ends in the UWOA upon cessation of hostilities or operations. Transition does not necessarily mean demobilization or the commencement of FID operations; however, it usually requires some form of stability operations.

Each application of unconventional warfare is unique. Phases may occur simultaneously or, in certain situations, not at all. For example, a large and effective resistance movement may require only logistical support, thereby bypassing the organization phase. The phases may also occur out of sequence, with each receiving varying degrees of emphasis. One example of this is when members of an irregular force are exfiltrated to a host nation to be trained and organized before infiltrating back into the UWOA, either with or without US SOF. In this case, the typical order of the phases would change.

CHAPTER 3
MARINE SPECIAL
OPERATIONS FORCES CHARACTERISTICS

The purpose of MARFORSOC is to provide expeditionary, task-organized, special operations forces for worldwide SOF operations. The Marine Corps' MAGTF concept of employment provides the foundation for MARFORSOC's organizational structure and capabilities; scalable SOF capable of executing independent operations against a wide range of adversaries, in any environment, under various conditions, to include time-sensitive crisis situations of a strategic nature. Marine Forces Special Operations Command's capability to integrate and task-organize MARSOF units with enhanced combat support and CSS structure, combined with the core strength of the MAGTF-style command and control provides the CDRUSSOCOM with options and depth for rapid response SOF capable of independent distributed operations.

The MAGTF mindset and robust SOF C2 systems enable MARSOF headquarters units to integrate and synchronize joint, coalition, and interagency forces into a single-battle concept for SOF operations within assigned areas of operations. Marine special operations forces' headquarters units vary in size ranging from Marine special operations company (MSOC), special operations task force (SOTF), and combined joint SOTF. These MARSOF headquarters units are organized and equipped to integrate all the warfighting functions in a holistic manner that achieve effects well above its "weight class."

Marine special operations forces consist of specially screened, assessed, selected, and trained Marines and Sailors to serve as MARSOF special operations officers (SOOs) and critical skills operators (CSOs). Special operations capability specialists (SOCSs) are screened, selected, and trained to provide specific combat support to special operations. The reinforced MARFORSOC capability is further supported by organic CSS. The MARSOF individual is a mentally agile member of the ultimate adaptable team. They are capable of operating from the tactical to strategic levels simultaneously, holistically evaluating problems and challenges, comprehending the situation, and making critical decisions in an effective manner. They execute missions in largely unstructured and ambiguous environments, often including rapid and diverse changes in terrain, enemy, and climate. They understand the impact of their actions, their nonactions, the environments they operate in, and how to achieve enduring, desired effects. They comprehend the nature of complex issues and have the ability to understand, decide, and act within multiple nested levels of intent.

The relationship and shared identity with the Marine Corps enables interoperability between MARSOF and other Marine forces (MARFOR) with an emphasis on the skills necessary to expeditiously project special operations capabilities globally, the Marine Corps' foundational concept as an expeditionary scalable air-ground-logistic team. The MAGTF is capable of conducting the full range of operations in any clime and place in unison with USSOCOM's philosophy of deploying for purpose. In an era where engagement is vital to shaping the environment, the Marine Corps and USSOCOM, through a combination of special operations and forward-deployed forces, create a synergistic effect for stopping wars before they start.

The staffing, promotion policy, and the training and education of MARFORSOC personnel are spread across several entities. Synchronized staff and commander action is required to ensure MARFORSOC Marines have equitable promotion, retention, and training and education opportunities—all leading toward a progressive career path that builds upon experience and increases leadership responsibilities.

Focusing on individual development and maturing the character of Marines assigned to MARFORSOC is facilitated through the military personnel development process. This requires a holistic, systematic approach—one that views individual development from assessment and selection (A&S) to expiration of active service—in order to produce quality personnel and avoid gaps, inconsistency, and inefficiencies.

Military personnel development encompasses many different areas of analysis, management, and assessment. The COMMARFORSOC is the overall process owner and no one staff section or subordinate command owns every process. Therefore, military personnel development is a collective approach powered by collaboration, assessment, and understanding of higher intent, knowledge, and cross-talk with lateral organizations and is tempered by realistic allocation of scarce resources and priorities. Marine Forces Special Operations Command maintains the individual and collective characteristics that define SOF by conducting a rigorous recruiting, screening, assessment, and selection process. By recruiting those individuals who show the potential to demonstrate the qualities demanded of MARFORSOC during screening and assessment, MARFORSOC ensures that those selected to attend the individual training course (ITC) have the potential to complete a rewarding career as a Marine conducting special operations.

MARINE FORCES SPECIAL OPERATIONS COMMAND RECRUITING AND SCREENING

Service with MARFORSOC is a highly demanding assignment because of the unique undertakings of SOF. Marines recruited to MARFORSOC come from across the Marine Corps and must be individually mature, intelligent, mentally agile, determined, ethical, and physically fit in order to contribute to and collaborate as part of a team conducting independent operations. The MARFORSOC screening process is designed to identify those Marines who demonstrate the potential to succeed as MARSOF, steadfast in their resolution to accomplish the mission, and determined to excel with *Spiritus Invictus*—an unconquerable spirit.

Additional information regarding the prerequisites for a MARFORSOC SOO military occupational specialty (MOS) 0370 and CSO MOS 0372 can be found in Marine Corps Order 1200.18, *Military Occupational Specialties (MOS) Program Order*, and at the MARFORSOC recruiting website www.marsoc.com.

Marine Forces Special Operations Command is supported by the other Services in specific functional areas, with the majority of those billets falling within the health service support (HSS) fields. Those Service members from the US Navy and US Army assigned to MARFORSOC also receive the appropriate screening to ensure they are assigned to a billet within the Service members' qualifications and ability. During their assignment to MARFORSOC, they can expect a balance of operational tempo and professional military development scoped toward supporting both MARFORSOC and their specific Service's career progression programs.

MARINE FORCES SPECIAL OPERATIONS COMMAND ASSESSMENT AND SELECTION

The MARFORSOC assessment and selection process varies for each Marine depending on their specific MOS. Each MOS screens their Marines according to their standards and qualifications. Assessment and selection for SOOs and CSOs are structured to determine whether a candidate has the necessary attributes to successfully complete SOF entry level training and follow-on assignment to an operational unit.

Assessment and selection is competitive and selective. Both SOOs and CSOs must be complex problem-solvers who are comfortable working in an ambiguous environment. The MARFORSOC recruiters provide potential candidates with a recommended training guide designed to physically prepare them for the rigors of the selection process. However, it is the applicant's responsibility to ensure that they are prepared to meet the challenges—mentally, morally, and physically—of A&S.

ASSESSMENT AND SELECTION PHASES

Phase I of A&S enhances a Marine's physical fitness and psyche in preparation for phase II assessment. This phase also provides education and mentorship on the MARFORSOC's culture and missions assigned.

Phase II of A&S builds on the baseline established in phase I and completes the testing process. This phase is conducted off-site in order to provide a new, challenging environment.

Throughout both phases, the assessment uses individual and team events to rate 10 key attributes. The combination of these attributes embodies the type of Marine who will succeed at the ITC and as a future SOO/CSO. No single attribute carries more weight than another.

Marine Forces Special Operations Command assesses candidates in individual and team events to ensure they possess the desired attributes that are required of a SOO or CSO. The 10 attributes are—

- *Integrity*. Does the right thing even when no one is watching.
- *Effective Intelligence*. Solves practical problems when a "book solution" is not available. Learns and applies new skills to unusual problems by making sound and timely decisions.

- *Physical Ability*. Having the necessary physical attributes and functional fitness to do one's job and persevere under stress.
- *Adaptability*. Continuously evaluates information about the present situation and changes one's plans as the situation changes, always operating within commander's intent.
- *Initiative*. Goes beyond the scope of duties without having to be guided or told what to do.
- *Determination*. Sustains a high level of effort over long periods of time despite the situation.
- *Dependability*. Can be relied on to complete tasks correctly, on time, and without supervision.
- *Teamwork*. Works well within a team, large or small.
- *Interpersonal Skill*. Interacts and influences others with a minimum of unnecessary strife or friction.
- *Stress Tolerance*. Deals with ambiguous, dangerous, high pressure, and/or frustrating events while maintaining control of emotions, actions, composure, and effectiveness.

SELECTION PROCESS

The data gleaned from the A&S evaluation is provided to the board members, who complete the selection process. The results of each candidate's performance are compiled and reviewed. After the review of the candidates' packages by the instructor cadre, the commander's board conducts another in-depth review.

The board interviews candidates and gives recommendations to the MSOS commander on those candidates they feel possess the desired attributes of a SOO and CSO.

Marines selected for assignment to a SOO or CSO billet as a result of successful completion of A&S will be notified, and their next step is to begin the SOO/CSO training pipeline. Marines who are not selected may be invited to reapply to attend A&S at a later date.

Not all military professionals are suited for special operations assignments. No negative stigma is associated with those individuals not selected during A&S. All candidates that put forth an honest effort are commended for accepting the challenge to pursue a career in a demanding and competitive community.

SPECIAL OPERATIONS OFFICER

Officers assigned to lead a Marine special operations team (MSOT) attend both A&S and the ITC alongside the CSO candidates. Upon graduation from ITC, they are awarded the 0370 MOS and attend the Team Commander Course. Special operations officers are then assigned to a Marine Raider battalion for service as team commanders and other SOF billets as they continue to serve as Marine officers in the special operations community. The SOO assignments at MARFORSOC start as a team commander. As a SOO's career progresses the billets demand greater responsibility.

Assignments include billets at a MSOC, Marine Raider battalion, the Marine Raider Regiment, MSOS, MARFORSOC headquarters, and SOF billets external to the MARFORSOC.

CRITICAL SKILLS OPERATORS

Critical skills operators are the SOF tacticians assigned to MARFORSOC in operator billets at the team, company, and battalion levels. A Marine is designated a CSO upon selection at A&S and graduation from the ITC. The CSOs are awarded the 0372 MOS. Upon the completion of the Basic Language Course (BLC), CSOs are assigned to a Marine Raider battalion (see fig. 3-1). As

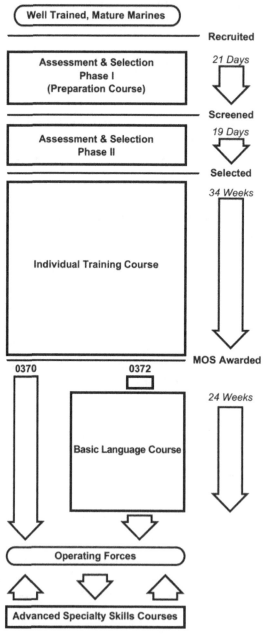

Figure 3-1. Special Operations Officer/Critical Skills Operator Training Pipeline.

a CSO's career progresses the billets demand greater responsibility. Assignments include billets at a MSOC, a Marine Raider battalion, the Marine Raider Regiment, MSOS, MARFORSOC headquarters, and SOF billets external to MARFORSOC.

SPECIAL OPERATIONS CAPABILITY SPECIALIST

The SOCS Marines are strategic and tactical force multipliers that directly support billets at the team, company, and battalion levels based on mission requirements. These Marines are recruited, screened, selected, and assigned to MARFORSOC based on their potential and MOS-associated skill sets. Upon assignment to MARFORSOC, SOCS attend a specialized MARSOF training pipeline (see fig. 3-2) that imparts the skills necessary to operate in a special operations

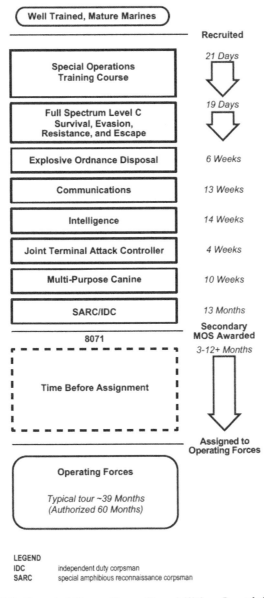

Figure 3-2. Special Operations Capabilities Specialist Pipeline.

environment. The SOCS occupational fields or specialties include, but are not limited to, intelligence, communications, EOD, canine handlers, and JTAC.

SPECIAL OPERATIONS COMBAT SERVICE SUPPORT

Marine Forces Special Operations Command units are further enabled with CSS Marines who are directly assigned to support billets at the company and battalion levels. Combat service support Marines work in their primary MOS in fields such as motor transport and logistics; they may also receive an appropriate level of SOF-related training as required to support their assigned operations.

The Marine Corps' philosophy and mindset of integrating the six warfighting functions, combined with MARSOF's enhanced command, control, communications, computers, and intelligence (C4I) systems and unique ability to task-organize, facilitate our core capability for command and control of small lethal expeditionary teams capable of executing complex distributed operations to achieve strategic effects. Marine special operations forces operational platforms include individual submersibles, inflatable maritime surface platforms, unmanned aircraft systems, and the family of SOF ground mobility vehicles. Marine Forces Special Operations Command's unique ability to task-organize with combat support and CSS Marines enables MARFORSOC to provide infinitely adaptable SOF with unmatched agility capable of conducting sustained distributed operations in austere and complex environments.

The MARFORSOC aligns billets with the USSOCOM operating force categories by managing capabilities and training in accordance with personnel types and skill areas. See table 3-1 on page 3-8.

MARINE SPECIAL OPERATIONS FORCES CAPABILITIES

Marine special operations forces personnel are trained, organized, and equipped to accomplish special operations in different environments, under arduous conditions, and with varying degrees of political sensitivity. These operations are accomplished through mastery of the SOF core activities and supporting tasks. Methods of insertion and extraction include amphibious surface and subsurface platforms; fixed-wing, tiltrotor, and rotary-wing aircraft; as well as ground mobility platforms. The method of insertion and extraction that best supports the mission will be determined during mission analysis. Capable of operating in all environments and conditions, MARSOF conduct individual, collective, mission-specific training and preparation that focuses on the application of the SOF core activities and supporting tasks, taking into account mission-specific operational conditions, geographic environment, and anticipated threats for the specified area of operations. The MARFORSOC trains, equips, and deploys task-organized and scalable elements that are full-spectrum, multidisciplinary forces tailored for commander, theater special operations (CDRTSOC) requirements.

Table 3-1. MARFORSOC Capabilities Categorization.

USSOCOM Operating Force Category	MARFORSOC Personnel Type	MARFORSOC Specific Training	MARFORSOC Capabilities Manager
B	SOO	ITC CSO capabilities certification	MSOS or CO
B	CSO-A	ITC CSO capabilities certification	MSOS or CO
D	SOCS-B	JTAC	G-3
D	SOCS-C	MNOC	G-6
D	SOCS-D	MPC handler	MRSG
D	SOCS-E	MARFORSOC EOD	G-3
D	SOCS-F	MARFORSOC SIGINT	G-2
D	SOCS-G	MARFORSOC GIS	G-2
D	SOCS-H	MARFORSOC HUMINT	G-2
D	SOCS-I	MARFORSOC intelligence analyst	G-2

Legend
CO   company
GIS   geospatial information systems
HUMINT   human intelligence
MNOC   Marine Forces Special Operations Command (MARFORSOC) network operators course
MRSG   Marine Raider Support Group
SIGINT   signals intelligence

All Marine SOOs and CSOs are trained to conduct the full range of special operations activities assigned to MARFORSOC. Designated team members will maintain a greater degree of proficiency in the following additional skills that are resident in every MSOT:

- Special reconnaissance (to include technical surveillance operations and exploitation).
- Weapons employment (sniping, light, medium, and heavy US and foreign weapons, and joint fires).
- Regional expertise (to include specific language and cultural training).
- Communications (voice/video/data across multiple pathways and networks).
- Explosives (basic demolitions, applied explosive techniques, explosive breaching).
- Aviation and airborne operations (air assault/support, parachute, JTAC, and limited aerial delivery support).
- Dive/amphibious operations (open and closed circuit diving, small boat coxswain).
- Ground mobility (advanced driving of and basic mechanic skills on multiple platforms).
- Special and environmental skills (e.g., military mountaineering, jungle warfare, amphibious, littoral, urban).
- Intelligence operations (to include sensitive site exploitation).

The five SOF truths identified in chapter 1 are based on historical experience and should be seen as an integrated and interwoven set of truths upon which MARSOF builds its capabilities. These truths also imply limitations for SOF employment, including MARSOF.

Due to high demand, SOF is typically deployed for specific purposes to provide a desired effect. Improper employment of MARSOF for nonspecial operations, applications, or missions is not recommended and highly discouraged on all occasions. The MARSOF requires external augmentation or support to offset limitations in the following areas:

- Platform support for insertion, extraction, and resupply.
- Fires, mobility, and CSS beyond limited organic capability/capacity.
- Sustained, tactical-level, Service-common and special operations-peculiar logistic support.

This Page Intentionally Left Blank

CHAPTER 4
MARINE FORCES SPECIAL
OPERATIONS COMMAND ORGANIZATION

MARINE FORCES SPECIAL OPERATIONS COMMAND CHAIN OF COMMAND

Marine Forces Special Operations Command is the Marine Corps SOF component under the combatant command of, and reporting directly to, CDRUSSOCOM. Marine Forces Special Operations Command is commanded by a Marine major general (O-8). The COMMARFORSOC exercises administrative control (ADCON) over all MARSOF in accordance with CDRUSSOCOM and Commandant of the Marine Corps guidance.

The COMMARFORSOC exercises OPCON, delegated by CDRUSSOCOM, over all US-based MARSOF. For Marine Corps-specific administrative and other matters, COMMARFORSOC reports directly to the Commandant as a MARFOR commander. Figure 4-1, on page 4-2, depicts MARFORSOC organization.

MARINE FORCES SPECIAL OPERATIONS COMMAND HEADQUARTERS ORGANIZATION

The MARFORSOC headquarters is located at Camp Lejeune, North Carolina. The headquarters staff consists of a functionally specific general staff system that supports COMMARFORSOC and a special staff operating under the direct cognizance of the MARFORSOC chief of staff. Figure 4-2, on page 4-3, depicts MARFORSOC headquarters organization.

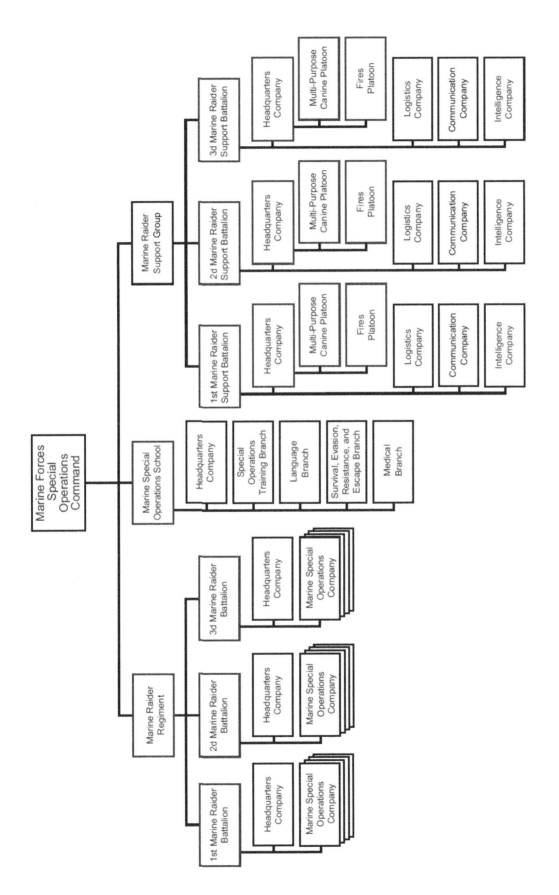

Figure 4-1. Marine Forces Special Operations Command Organization.

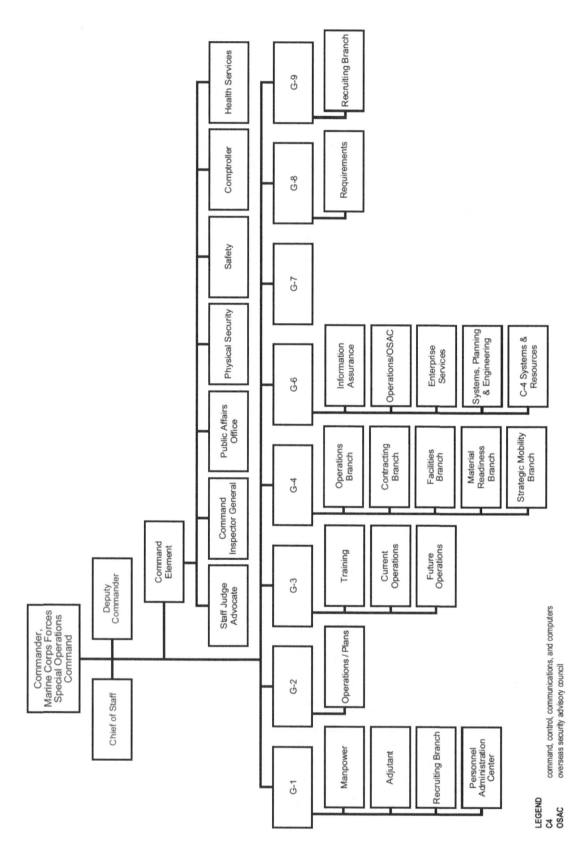

Figure 4-2. Marine Forces Special Operations Command Headquarters Organization.

LEGEND
C4   command, control, communications, and computers
OSAC overseas security advisory council

MARINE RAIDER REGIMENT ORGANIZATION

The Marine Raider Regiment is a subordinate command of MARFORSOC that is capable of planning, conducting, and supporting special operations in all operational environments. Located at Camp Lejeune, North Carolina, the regiment is commanded by a command-selected, Marine colonel (O-6). The regiment provides a balanced force comprised of a regimental staff and 3 Raider battalions consisting of 12 special operations companies that are further divided into 48 special operations teams. Marine Corps Reference Publication (MCRP) 1-10.1, *Organization of the United States Marine Corps*, depicts Marine Raider Regiment organization.

The Marine Raider Regiment's mission is to train, structure, equip, and deploy specially-qualified MARSOF to conduct worldwide special operations missions as directed by the COMMARFORSOC. The Marine Raider Regiment roles and responsibilities are as follows:

- Train, educate, equip, support, and deploy assigned MARSOF capable of executing the SOF core activities of direct action, special reconnaissance, SFA, counterterrorism, FID, COIN, support of CWMD, and support to unconventional warfare.
- Perform command functions for assigned forces including readiness evaluations and automated information system support to the staff and subordinate commands. Support subordinate units with message dissemination; financial management; medical, legal, and chaplain services; safety; explosive safety; and travel orders processing.
- Plan, coordinate, and conduct unilateral, joint, and combined special operations and exercises as directed.
- Establish the nucleus of and function as a combined task force and/or joint special operations task force for contingency operations or major theater exercises as directed, while maintaining required basic command functions in garrison.
- Provide forces to support exercises and operations as required.
- Provide input to support COMMARFORSOC's planning, programming, budgeting, and execution system requirements, in coordination with MARFORSOC G-1 and G-8.
- Develop, test, and validate collective-level MARSOF TTP in coordination with MARFORSOC G-7, Marine Special Operations School, and Marine Raider Support Group.
- Support MARFORSOC planning as directed.
- Maintain visibility and accountability of assets through coordinated management of the table of organic allowance.
- Continue to exercise ADCON of MARSOF deployed from the Marine Raider Regiment.
- Manage and sustain regional language requirements.

MARINE RAIDER BATTALION

Marine Raider Battalion Mission

The Marine Raider battalion trains, sustains, and maintains combat readiness, deploys and employs task-organized MARSOF to conduct the full range of special operations assigned to COMMARFORSOC in support of CDRUSSOCOM and/or the GCCs.

Marine Raider Battalion Roles and Responsibilities

Marine Raider battalions perform the full range of SOF core activities and operations assigned to MARFORSOC. These activities include, but are not limited to, counterterrorism, COIN, FID/SFA, direct action, special reconnaissance, and support of CWMD and unconventional warfare. The battalions must also train, plan for, and provide forces to execute battalion-level C2 functions such as those typically required for SOTF operations. Additionally, the battalions provide cryptographic material security support to its subordinate elements.

Marine Raider Battalion Organization

Marine Raider battalions are subordinate commands to the Marine Raider Regiment and are commanded by command-selected, Marine lieutenant colonels (O-5). Each battalion is organized into a fully functional headquarters staff with a headquarters and service company and four MSOCs. Marine Corps Reference Publication 1-10.1 depicts the Marine Raider battalion organization.

Marine Special Operations Company Organization

The MSOC is a scalable, task-organized unit commanded by a Marine, SOO-qualified major (O-4) that deploys in support of SOF specific tasking. The MSOC conducts special operations in austere, politically-sensitive environments for extended periods of time due to its special insertion and extraction skills, its combat support, and its CSS capabilities. The MSOC is capable of integrated find, fix, finish, exploit, analyze, and disseminate (F3EAD) operations, either unilaterally or bilaterally through partner/surrogate/HN forces. It is capable of distributed C4I over long distance in ambiguous environments. The headquarters of an MSOC can perform as an expeditionary intelligence fusion cell; as such, it can provide all-source intelligence analysis, collection, fusion, and processing, exploitation and dissemination; target package development, mission planning, and command of SOF operations; command and control and fires coordination for combat operations; coordination and information sharing with adjacent units; exploitation analysis center support to F3EAD; and support to TSOC campaign plans. The MSOC is task-organized and designed to achieve tactical and operational results that are strategically relevant and capable of deploying task-organized expeditionary SOF to conduct operations in support of the GCCs. Figure 4-3, on page 4-6, depicts the typical organization of an MSOC broken down to the element level.

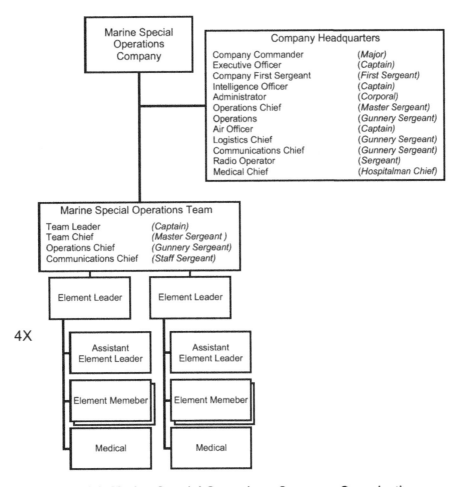

Figure 4-3. Marine Special Operations Company Organization.

Marine Special Operations Team Organization

The MSOT is the base MARSOF element consisting of 1 Marine SOO-qualified captain (O-3), 11 enlisted Marine CSOs, and 2 Navy corpsmen. An MSOT may deploy as part of an MSOC or independently in support of other SOF headquarters. When conducting special operations, the MSOT may be employed unilaterally or bilaterally in conjunction with other SOF units, other government agencies, or integrated with conventional forces for an extended period of time with limited external support. The MSOT possesses a baseline capability to task-organize based on mission requirements and deploy into austere environments via special insertion and extraction skills. The MSOT possesses the capability to conduct special long-range communications and advanced information gathering. The MSOT is capable of integrated F3EAD either unilaterally or bilaterally through partner/surrogate/HN forces. The MSOT is prepared to conduct decentralized operations in austere politically sensitive, hostile, or denied environments. The MSOT is capable of limited independent and split team operations, designed to achieve tactical and operational results that are strategically relevant. The MSOT is designed to include additional training per element to include engineering, weapons, operations/intelligence, communications, and medical.

MARINE RAIDER SUPPORT GROUP

Marine Raider Support Group Organization

The Marine Raider Support Group is a subordinate command of MARFORSOC that trains, equips, structures, and provides specifically-qualified Marine forces, including, but not limited to, logistics, intelligence, MPC, firepower control teams, and communications support to sustain worldwide special operations missions as directed by COMMARFORSOC. Located at Camp Lejeune, North Carolina, the support group is commanded by a command-selected, Marine colonel (O-6). The organization of the Marine Raider Support Group, as depicted in MCRP 1-10.1, reflects the habitual supporting relationships between the support battalions and the battalions within the Marine Raider Regiment. The Marine Raider Support Group's support battalions house the various functional teams tasked to support special operations requirements, providing MARFORSOC the span of organic support capabilities that make it unique. Through its subordinate units, the support group provides general support, direct support, combat support, and CSS support to MARFORSOC and its subordinate units.

Marine Raider Support Group Mission

Marine Raider Support Group trains, sustains, and maintains combat readiness and deploys specially-qualified Marine combat support and CSS forces to support MARSOF worldwide and provide garrison functions for the MARFORSOC.

Marine Raider Support Group Roles and Responsibilities

The Marine Raider Support Group roles and responsibilities are as follows:

- Train, support, and maintain combat readiness and provide combat support and CSS to support MARSOF or as directed by COMMARFORSOC.
- Perform command functions for assigned forces including readiness evaluations and automated information system support to the staff and subordinate commands. Support subordinate units with message dissemination; financial management; medical, legal, and chaplain services; safety; explosive safety; and travel orders processing.
- Support MARSOF with requisite combat support and CSS during planning, coordination, and conduct of unilateral, joint, and combined special operations and exercises as required.
- Provide garrison functions for the MARFORSOC headquarters to include administration, facilities, health services, ordnance, and supply.
- Provide combat support and CSS to support MARSOF training as required.
- Provide input to support COMMARFORSOC's planning, programming, budgeting, and execution system requirements.
- Support MARFORSOC planning as required/directed.
- Maintain accountability of assets through coordinated management of the table of allowance.

MARINE RAIDER SUPPORT BATTALION

Support Battalion Mission and Tasks
The support battalions train, sustain, and maintain combat readiness and perform change of OPCON for the deployment of specially-qualified Marine combat support and CSS capabilities in support of special operations worldwide.

Support Battalion Organization
The support battalions are Marine Raider Support Group subordinate commands located at Camp Lejeune, North Carolina, and Camp Pendleton, California. Command-selected, Marine lieutenant colonels (O-5) command the battalions. Support battalions contain headquarters and service, communications, intelligence, and logistic companies. Each of these companies organizes, trains, and equips teams to support special operations requirements and is oriented to support an associated Marine Raider battalion.

Communications Company Organization
Each communications company organizes, trains, and equips three command, control, communications, and computer support teams (C4STs). These teams are trained to provide high-bandwidth voice, video, and data services to the MSOC headquarters and MSOTs.

Intelligence Company Organization
Each intelligence company organizes, trains, and equips an intelligence support team and three direct support teams (DSTs). These teams are comprised of SOCS who are trained to conduct intelligence activities and operations in support of special operations missions in politically sensitive, hostile, or denied areas, using mission appropriate means of collection, analysis, and reporting.

The intelligence support team is specifically configured to provide intelligence support at the Marine Raider battalion or special operations command-forward (SOC-FWD) level and routinely forms the core of the intelligence capability for the assigned unit. The DST is the smallest intelligence support unit and is specifically configured to provide intelligence support at the MSOC-level. Although organized for support at the company level, the DST is able to subdivide into smaller direct support elements to provide intelligence support down to the MSOT level, MARFORSOC's smallest deployable tactical unit.

Logistic Company Organization
Each logistic company organizes, trains, and equips three logistics support teams (LSTs). These teams are assigned in support of deploying Marine Raider battalions to provide logistical support coordination, maintenance, and general CSS.

MARINE SPECIAL OPERATIONS SCHOOL

The mission of MSOS is to assess and select personnel for assignment for MARFORSOC and to train and educate designated personnel in individual, basic, and advanced special operations in order to meet MARFORSOC's requirement to provide personnel to conduct special operations.

The MSOS is a subordinate command of MARFORSOC that trains and educates Marines and Sailors for special operations assignments. The school provides advanced individual special operations training; plans and executes the component deployment certification exercise; and serves as the MARFORSOC education proponent. Located at Camp Lejeune, North Carolina, the school is commanded by a command-selected, Marine colonel (O-6). The MSOS commander exercises OPCON and ADCON of subordinate commanders and assigned forces for COMMARFORSOC. The current organization structure for MSOS is depicted in of MCRP 1-10.1.

Marine Special Operations School roles and responsibilities are as follows:

- Conduct individual and basic training.
- Conduct advanced special operations training.
- Conduct language and cultural training.
- Introduce and reinforce MARFORSOC Preservation of the Force and Family (MPOTFF).
- Coordinate, via component, with Joint Special Operations University and Training and Education Command for higher level and Service training and education.
- Develop and introduce, as the component lead, special operations TTP in coordination with component, Marine Raider Regiment, and Marine Raider Support Group.
- Perform required curriculum review and updates of training material for all assigned courses.

The MSOS is MARFORSOC's formal learning center that conducts initial and advanced training courses, providing additional capabilities to individual CSOs and combat support personnel, resulting in a comprehensive capability at the unit level. The ITC is a 9-month training pipeline that produces standards-based, qualified CSOs and SOOs respectively (see fig. 4-4 on page 4-10). Combat support personnel attend a training pipeline for approximately 6 months depending upon MOS.

Training and Education Branch

The Training and Education Branch provides oversight to ensure MSOS courses are conducted in accordance with approved programs of instruction and that the programs of instruction are reviewed and updated in accordance with applicable orders; conducts and documents instructor training, certification, and evaluation; and provides continuity of student welfare throughout their attendance at all MSOS courses. This branch also manages the execution of phase 0 of the ITC which encompasses in-processing; communications; medical; and survival, evasion, resistance, and escape (SERE).

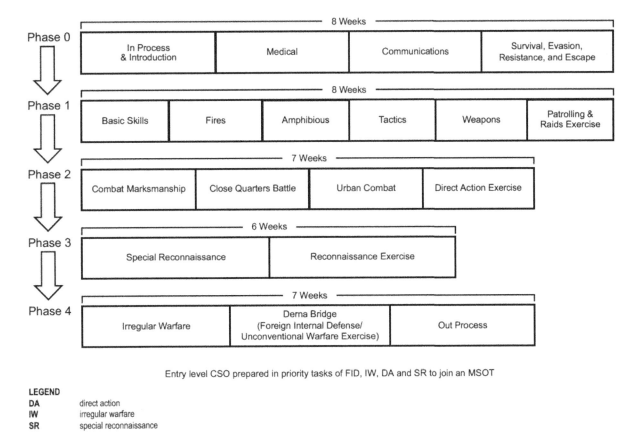

Figure 4-4. Individual Training Course Phases.

Special Skills Branch
The Special Skills Branch is responsible for the execution of the SERE and BLCs.

Survival, Evasion, Resistance, and Escape
The SERE course provides formal training and instruction for MARFORSOC's institutional SERE requirements to include risk of isolation, full-spectrum level C, and peacetime government detention/hostage detention.

Language
The BLC, overseen by the Special Skills Branch, is an intensive language acquisition program designed to produce qualified linguists. The BLC currently focuses on the following MARFORSOC core languages: Arabic, French (Sub-Saharan), Indonesian, and Tagalog. Future adjustments in MARFORSOC's regional focus areas will guide additional development of language and cultural training conducted by MSOS.

Assessment and Selection Branch
The A&S Branch conducts the A&S program. These programs screen, assess, and select Marines for future service as MARSOF. The A&S Branch has the responsibility of preparing Marines for ITC as well as assessing their potential for successful service as a SOO or CSO.

Special Operations Training Companies

Training at the MSOS is conducted by the special operations training companies (SOTCs). The SOTCs are responsible for the execution of specific phases of ITC; tasked with the execution of advanced courses; and provide support to SOO, CSO, and SOCS training pipelines. The SOTC assignments as it pertains to ITC and advanced courses are listed below—

- SOTC-1, ITC Phase One: MARSOF Heliborne Insertion and Extraction Training (MHIET).
- SOTC-2, ITC Phase Two: MARSOF Master Breacher Course (MMBC), MARSOF Close Quarters Battle Leaders 2 Course (MCQBL2).
- SOTC-3, ITC Phase Three: Special Reconnaissance, MARSOF Technical Surveillance Course (MTSC), MARSOF Advance Sniper Course (MASC), Advanced Special Operations Techniques Level II (ASOT II).
- SOTC-4, ITC Phase Four: Team Commanders Course (TCC).

Further details on the assessment and selection phases and training pipelines are contained in chapter 7.

This Page Intentionally Left Blank

CHAPTER 5
MARINE FORCES SPECIAL OPERATIONS COMMAND COMMAND AND CONTROL

Marine SOF are instilled with the Marine Corps' integrative approach to building task-organized forces, as seen in MAGTFs, and a historical familiarity with amphibious and expeditionary operating environments. Marine Forces Special Operations Command's small wars heritage and MAGTF mentality drive heavy emphasis on well-developed intelligence, gained by employing all-source intelligence professionals down to the team level, while supporting robust C2 capabilities at all levels. This makes MARFORSOC well-suited for the full range of special operations, activities, and tasks.

THE MARFORSOC EMPLOYMENT MODEL

The MARFORSOC concept of employment (see fig. 5-1 on page 5-2) is a result of current and emerging mission tasks and predictive analysis. To be effective, MARFORSOC develops a special operations operator supported by integrated combat support and CSS. The outcome is a force comprised of full-spectrum SOF personnel—personnel who understand the impact of their actions and are able to address underlying socioeconomic and political situations across the range of military operations.

Several references guide MARFORSOC strategic appreciation of global issues and employment. The following national security and Service documents influence the operational and training vision of MARFORSOC:

- The National Military Strategy of the United States of America 2015.
- Guidance for Employment of the Force 2015-2017.
- JP 3-05.
- USSOCOM Directive 10-1cc Terms of Reference–Roles, Missions, and Functions of Component Commands.
- USSOCOM Capabilities and Programming Guidance (2017–2021).
- USSOCOM posture statement by Admiral William H. McRaven (2013).
- USSOCOM Commander's Memorandum for Education and Training Guidance, FY 2013–2016.
- Joint Operating Concept for Irregular Warfare: Countering Irregular Threats v2.0.
- Naval Operations Concept 2010.
- Marine Corps Concepts and Programs April 2016.

- Marine Corps Doctrinal Publication (MCDP) 1, *Warfighting.*
- Marine Corps Warfighting Publication (MCWP) 3-02, *Insurgencies and Countering Insurgencies.*

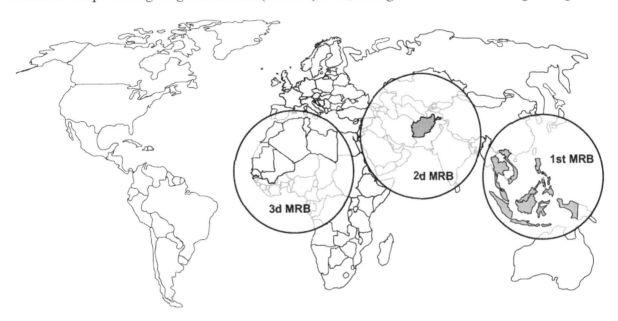

3 x subregionally-focused Marine Raider battalions

   • Each aligned to a TSOC (USAFRICOM, USCENTCOM, USPACOM)
   • MRBs maintain planning/coordination relationship with aligned TSOC

1 x MSOC (rein) per subregion

   • OPCON to the TSOC
   • Enabled execution of all MARSOC core operations/activities
   • Maintain persistent/consistent presence, including country team representation

LEGEND	
USAFRICOM	United States Africa Command
USCENTCOM	United States Central Command
USPACOM	United States Pacific Command

Figure 5-1. MARFORSOC Concept of Employment and Regional Alignment.

MISSION TYPE ORDERS

Mission type orders are the ultimate expression of decentralized execution; however, they can only be fully optimized with an understanding and appreciation of commander's intent two levels up the chain of command, and the linkage to desired operational and strategic effects. Marine special operations forces leadership enables this execution, even in missions of tremendous risk and importance. Given from higher headquarters, the mission type order and accompanying commander's intent provide the subordinate leader at each level with an overarching mission but leave the planning and execution method to the subordinate leader. Much of the freedom of movement, specificity of effort, and specified and implied tasks are developed at the lowest level of execution. Significant effort and emphasis is placed on initiative, experience, and ultimately trust—in the leader and in the training system—based on a comprehensive understanding of commander's intent two levels up the chain of command.

A characteristic of MARSOF is its ability to conduct distributed operations at the smallest element level—fully capable of operating independently. The high degree of training, coupled with small unit leadership and team cohesion, gives the MARSOF an innate ability to provide effects across a wide region.

Due to the nature of special operations, missions are conducted during all of the joint operational phases. The MARSOF elements must be prepared to transition in-stride from shaping efforts to high-intensity lethal operations. The leader and the subordinate elements will ensure execution is accomplished across the full range of operations through the method of mission type orders.

In some instances, the MARFORSOC operators will find themselves in a rapidly developing situation with an absence of tactical-level orders. These situations will often be beyond those encountered on the typical battlefield. It is then that the Marine will rely upon those intangible qualities as he/she assesses the situation with a thorough understanding of the mission and the effects of the decisions and actions.

THEATER SPECIAL OPERATIONS COMMAND

The first TSOCs were formed in the mid-1980s. The TSOC is the SOF subordinate unified command within the geographic combatant command. As the primary theater SOF organization, they are capable of performing broad continuous special operations missions and other activities. The CDRTSOC has three principal roles: as a JFC, to plan and conduct joint operations as directed by the GCC; as the theater special operations advisor to the GCC and other component commanders; and as the joint force special operations component commander (JFSOCC) when the GCC establishes functional component commanders for operations, absent the establishment of a JTF. Through a deliberate process of analysis, the TSOCs list future SOF requirements validated by the GCC to execute peacetime/pre-crisis phase 0 and phase 1 activities.

This relationship between the GCC and TSOC improves coordination, SOF capacity, resources, capabilities, and communications among the deployed MARSOF elements and other forces operating in the geographic region through a clear set of authorities managed by the TSOC.

SPECIAL OPERATIONS COMMAND-FORWARD

The SOC-FWD is a smaller command element located elsewhere in the theater of operation. Typically smaller than a TSOC, the SOC-FWD is tasked to provide command and control of SOF and synchronize efforts among the country team, HN forces, multinational forces and agencies as required.

As a task-organized headquarters, it provides a forward-deployed presence for operational command and control. The SOC-FWD is scalable and command tailored to the appropriate level of command and control for the situation. As an operation matures, the SOC-FWD may expand to multiple SOTFs or form the core of a JSOTF or special operations joint task force (commonly referred to as SOJTF). If a more robust SOF capability is required, the SOC-FWD may transition to a JSOTF.

SPECIAL OPERATIONS JOINT TASK FORCE

A special operations joint task force is established to improve conventional forces/SOF integration and interdependence. Acting as a headquarters to plan and coordinate theater-level special operations, the special operations joint task force provides command and control over the employment and sustainment of US and multinational SOF. The purpose of the special operations joint task force is to synchronize the warfighting functions while improving efficiencies in manpower, and enabling capabilities and coordination to all special operations in theater.

JOINT SPECIAL OPERATIONS TASK FORCE

A joint special operations task force is comprised of two or more units from the SOF Service components. A joint special operations task force is normally established by a subordinate unified commander such as a CDRTSOC or commander, joint task force (CJTF). When the JSOTF is formed it is normally comprised with staff from the TSOC and augmented by Service components or an existing O-6-level headquarters from an existing SOF Service component, with augmentation from special operations or conventional forces.

SPECIAL OPERATIONS TASK FORCE

When SOF requires additional command and control, a temporary SOTF can be established to provide the required warfighting functions. Marine Forces Special Operations Command is capable of supporting the requirement with a sustained presence supported from the Marine Raider battalions. The task-organized SOTF will facilitate joint SOF operations and integration in the joint area of operation. The SOTF will provide command and control for the SOF elements, a line of communication to the TSOC, and coordination with conventional forces, agencies, and partners.

LIAISON ELEMENTS

As required, SOF will provide liaison elements to coordinate, deconflict, and synchronize special operations and activities with conventional forces and other agencies. The liaison element is task-organized and ranges in size from a single SOF operator to a team-size element. Requirements include, but are not limited to, providing liaison to joint commands, air components, host nations, and US agencies and departments.

COMMAND RELATIONSHIPS WITHIN A GEOGRAPHIC COMBATANT COMMAND

While in the continental United States, SOF is under the combatant command (command authority) of CDRUSSOCOM. When directed, CDRUSSOCOM provides US-based SOF to the GCCs. The GCCs normally exercise combatant command (command authority) of assigned and OPCON of attached SOF through the CDRTSOC.

Marine Forces Special Operations Command does not permanently assign forces to the GCCs. All MARSOF are based in the continental United States and deploy in accordance with joint staff guidance articulated through USSOCOM via the Global Force Management Process. Deployed MARSOF are transferred for specified periods and support the GCCs employing SOF with OPCON exercised through their respective TSOCs. Figure 5-2 depicts the standard command relationships (and authorities) for MARSOF supporting a GCC.

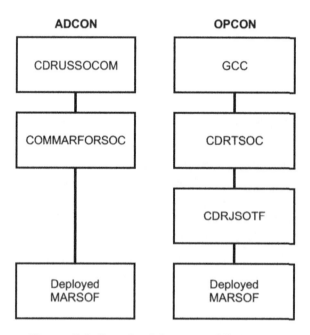

Figure 5-2. Standard Command Relationships.

As illustrated, COMMARFORSOC retains ADCON of deployed MARSOF. In addition to being the primary mechanism by which a GCC exercises command and control over SOF, the TSOC is the primary theater SOF organization.

When a JFC (GCC or CJTF) establishes and employs subordinate JTFs and independent task forces, the CDRTSOC may establish and employ multiple JSOTFs to command and control SOF capabilities and accommodate the separate JTF/task force special operations requirements. Figure 5-3 depicts these organizations and command relationships. Accordingly, the GCC/CJTF, as the establishing authority and common commander, will normally establish the desired command relationships, typically supporting or tactical control, between the respective CJTFs/ task force commanders and their commanders, joint special operations task force (CDRJSOTFs).

Depending on the particular situation and establishing authorities, there are several different command relationships regarding SOF within a GCC's AOR—

- The GCC may directly exercise OPCON over all SOF.
- A GCC will typically designate a CDRTSOC/JFSOCC to exercise OPCON over designated CDRJSOTFs.
- The JFC, subordinate to the GCC (i.e., a CJTF) may exercise OPCON over CDRJSOTFs, potentially through a subordinate JFSOCC.
- The CDRJSOTF may exercise OPCON over subordinate CDRJSOTFs and typically exercises OPCON over their SOF Service component forces.

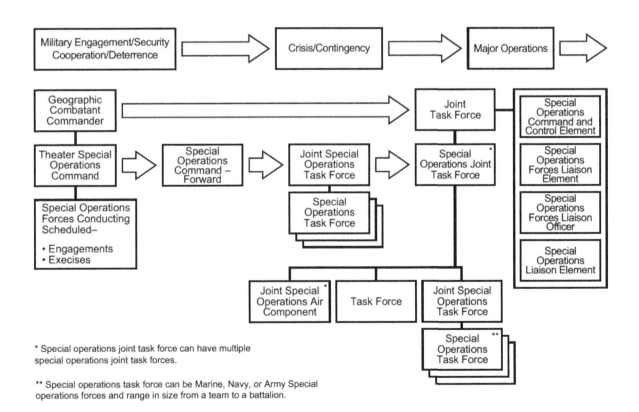

* Special operations joint task force can have multiple special operations joint task forces.

** Special operations task force can be Marine, Navy, or Army Special operations forces and range in size from a team to a battalion.

Figure 5-3. Command and Control of Special Operations Forces in Theater.

Regardless of the command relationship under which SOF operates, SOF is most effective when fully integrated and synchronized into an overall plan. Given the ability of SOF to operate unilaterally and independently as part of the overall plan, or in support of a conventional forces commander, effective coordination and integration of SOF is dependent on a clearly defined C2 structure. Successful execution of special operations requires centralized, responsive, and unambiguous command and control.

REGIONALIZATION

Marine Forces Special Operations Command's concept of employment is executed through a regionally aligned, persistent engagement, which further supports C2 habitual relationships with the TSOC and GCC. Focusing on the identified regions, MARFORSOC builds capability supported by regional experience and cultural knowledge. This concept supports the GCC's requirements while building component awareness with the degree of fidelity only developed over time. This method allows MARSOF to establish and mature relationships and networks with US-friendly governments and groups. Potential operating environments will be prepared through building partner capability and capacity from the persistent forward-deployed posture. Typically, command and control of MARSOF will be provided by the regional TSOC; in those cases where additional command and control is required, temporary C2 structure (e.g., a SOTF) can be provided from the USSOCOM components.

THE MARINE SPECIAL OPERATIONS COMPANY (REINFORCED)

The Marine special operations company (reinforced) (MSOC [rein]) is task-organized for deployment and employment from capabilities resident within the Marine Raider Regiment and Marine Raider Support Group. An MSOC (rein) is capable of conducting special operations in austere environments for extended periods of time due to the integration of combat support and logistic capabilities. The MSOC (rein) is capable of conducting full-spectrum SOF missions assigned by the GCC via the TSOC. These missions include integrated F3EAD operations, either unilaterally or bilaterally through partner/surrogate/HN forces.

Marine Special Operations Company (Reinforced) Tasks
Marine special operations company (rein) tasks are as follows:

- Command and control, plan, coordinate, and execute designated special operations missions with organic and attached units. Execute distributed C4I over long distances in ambiguous environments, including command and control of joint and partner nation SOF units.
- Conduct the following core activities: direct action, special reconnaissance, counterterrorism, FID/SFA, COIN, support to CWMD, and support to unconventional warfare. Support SOF core activities of hostage rescue and recovery, foreign humanitarian assistance, MISO, and CAO, as required. The MSOC (rein) personnel are capable of executing special insertion and extraction methods as required to support core activities execution.

- Conduct intelligence activities and operations in support of special operations missions in politically-sensitive, hostile, or denied areas, using mission appropriate means of collection, analysis, and reporting, either unilaterally or bilaterally through partner, paramilitary, resistance, surrogate, irregular and/or HN forces.
- Conduct special activities and PE in accordance with authorities in support of theater taskings.
- Train and equip subordinate MSOTs for individual deployment/employment. The MSOTs can be task-organized with intelligence, communications, and other enabling capabilities and are trained to individually accomplish all assigned core activities, to include the conduct of full-spectrum F3EAD operations to support distributed employment.

Marine Special Operations Company (Reinforced) Organization

The MSOC (rein) consists of a task-organized company headquarters section and four MSOTs. The MSOC headquarters section consists of specific personnel necessary to command and control the four MSOTs, provide combat support and limited logistic support, and coordinate CSS for organic and attached forces (see fig. 5-4 on page 5-9).

The MSOT is the base unit within the MSOC for execution of special operations missions and activities. It consists of 14 Marines and Sailors and can be task-organized and enabled with combat support and logistic attachments to provide enhanced capabilities for the execution of such missions.

The MSOC (rein) is task-organized with the following and other combat support and logistic attachments as determined by mission analysis for a respective deployment:

- The C4STs enable base MARSOF elements (MSOC and MSOT) and provide SOF information enterprise voice, video, and data network services.
- The DST deploys with an MSOC (rein) as its intelligence capability. The DSTs are able to task-organize into multiple direct support elements with the ability to provide collection and analysis capabilities at the MSOT level or for independent intelligence operations as directed by the supported commander.
- The LST is tasked and designed to plug into the theater logistic support structure to coordinate MSOC logistic support through the TSOC. The MSOC organic logistic capabilities can include limited ammunition support, embarkation; field-level/operator maintenance on boats, communications; generator, motor transport, and ordnance equipment; parachute rigging; and supply.
- The SOF EOD technicians enhance the MSOC with capabilities that include support and leadership of counterimprovised explosive device efforts, technical support and technical surveillance, sensitive site exploitation, and MARFORSOC support to theater CWMD efforts.
- The JTACs provide firepower planning, coordination, and control capabilities for application of aviation, direct and indirect, conventional, and USSOCOM-unique fires.
- MPC operations (on and off leash) include explosives detection, human-tracking operations, and lethal attack, as well as MPC mission planning, and support to external agencies.

To prepare a cohesive SOF team for employment by the TSOC and GCC, the base MSOC and its supporting elements combine to form an MSOC (rein) 180 days prior to deployment.

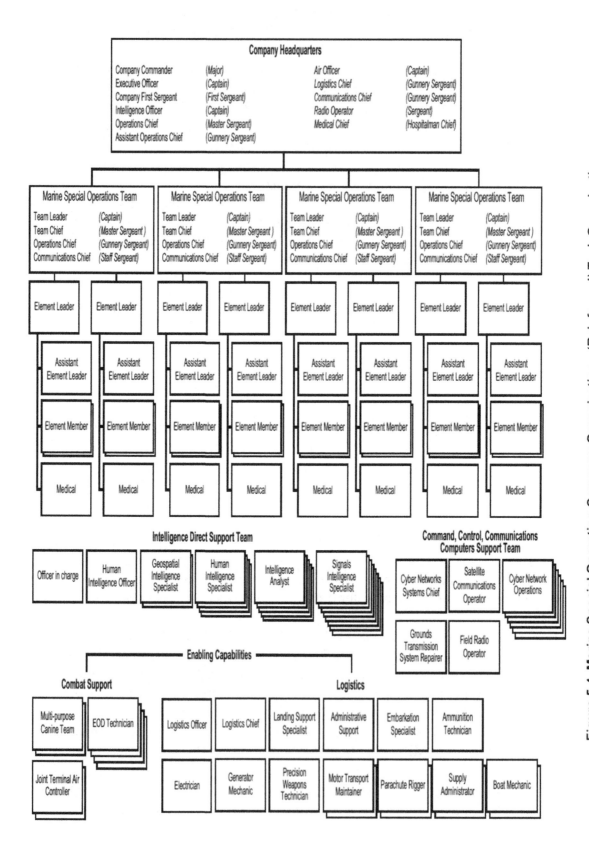

Figure 5-4. Marine Special Operation Company Organizations (Reinforced) Task Organization.

The headquarters of an MSOC (rein) can perform as an expeditionary intelligence fusion cell. As such, it can provide all-source intelligence analysis, collection, fusion, and processing; exploitation and dissemination; target package development, mission planning and command of SOF operations; command and control and fires coordination for combat operations; coordination and information sharing with adjacent units; exploitation analysis center support to F3EAD; and support to TSOC campaign plans.

Reinforced MSOCs also contain Marines trained in specialized collateral duties (e.g., pay agent, field ordering officer, hazardous materials, contracting officer's representative, jumpmaster) and are capable of attaching, employing, and supporting other SOF and conventional force capabilities such as MISO, information operations, cyberspace operations, and electronic warfare as available or required.

Marine Special Operations Company (Reinforced) Capabilities

Maneuver. Each MSOC (rein) deploys task-organized, scalable, and expeditionary Marine SOF to its aligned theater to accomplish the full range of special operations missions. When task-organized, the MSOC headquarters is capable of planning, directing, and coordinating assigned forces in the execution of special operations missions in support of the CDRUSSOCOM and/or the GCC employing SOF. The MSOCs (rein) elements are capable of motorized and dismounted operations across all operational environments. When needed by the operation, elements of the MSOC (rein) are capable of conducting operations that require specialized environmental mobility (mountain, jungle, desert, cold weather, littorals, airborne). Elements of the MSOC are also readily transportable by boats, tracked and wheeled vehicles, helicopters, ships, landing craft, and nonstandard or indigenous vehicles.

Fires. Organic firepower consists of individual weapons; light, medium, and heavy machine guns; and mortars. The MSOC (rein) is capable of employing, coordinating, integrating, and deconflicting the full range of indirect and air-delivered fires in support of their operations. These activities include training, mission planning, battle damage reporting of aviation and other fires, and are directly related to USSOCOMs F3EAD targeting process.

Intelligence. When task-organized, the MSOC headquarters intelligence section provides intelligence support to subordinate and supported units through direction, planning, collection, production, and dissemination of mission-oriented products. The DST enables the MSOC to conduct integrated all-source intelligence operations (planning, collection, analysis and fusion, production, dissemination, and utilization of intelligence products); intelligence, surveillance, and reconnaissance operations, including collections requirements and collections operations management; organic signals intelligence and special communications support; geospatial (topographic, hydrographic, imagery) intelligence analysis, fusion, and production; and counterintelligence/human intelligence operations.

Logistics. The LST is tasked and designed to plug into the theater logistic support structure to coordinate MSOC logistic support through the TSOC. Marine special operations company organic logistic capabilities can include supply; embarkation; parachute rigging; limited ammunition support; and field-level/operator maintenance on boats, communications, generators, motor transport, and ordnance equipment. Logistic support and CSS required beyond organic capability are attained through coordination with the TSOC.

Command and Control. The MSOC plans, directs, and coordinates the actions of the MSOC headquarters and its MSOTs to accomplish assigned missions and tasks. Once task-organized with a C4ST, the MSOC (rein) headquarters is able to command and control organic, joint, and combined SOF to accomplish the full range of special operations missions in support of the CDRUSSOCOM and/or the GCC employing SOF. The MSOC (rein) normally deploys with two, SOF-deployable, nodes-medium communications systems (one for operations, one for intelligence) and its associated supporting equipment, as well as three TOP SECRET intelligence nodes and two, SOF-deployable, nodes-light communications systems per MSOT. The MSOC (rein) and its organic MSOTs have the capability to communicate via multiple wideband voice, video, and data networks depending on the requirements of the mission. Missions requiring communications assets beyond organic capability are sourced through the Marine Raider Support Group or supported TSOC.

Force Protection. Each MSOC coordinates with subordinate units and the TSOC to plan and execute actions to protect US forces. The SOF EOD capabilities inherent to the enabled MSOC allow the force to support and lead counter-improvised explosive device efforts, technical support and technical surveillance, and sensitive site exploitation; the MSOC is further capable of providing support as directed to theater CWMD efforts. When deployed, the MSOC commander coordinates with the TSOC to plan and execute actions to provide force protection for assigned SOF.

Health Services. The MSOC (rein) deploys with SOF independent duty corpsmen (commonly referred to as IDCs) and special amphibious reconnaissance corpsmen (commonly referred to as SARCs) to provide advanced trauma life support for battle and non-battle casualties. Additionally, they are capable of providing organic minor dental; veterinary, preventive medicine, and operational stress control services; treatment of minor illnesses and injuries; physical therapy; and rehabilitation. Wounded, ill, and injured Service members requiring hospitalization are stabilized and transported to the nearest higher echelon of care facility (i.e., Role II or III).

Small Unmanned Aircraft Systems. Each MSOC (rein) deploys with eight collateral-duty, unmanned aircraft system operators embedded within the MSOTs. A MSOC (rein) deploys with a robust family of small, unmanned aircraft systems capable of conducting operations in most tactical, environmental, or atmospheric conditions in support of airborne intelligence, surveillance, and reconnaissance; command and control; control/observation of fires and maneuver; and force protection.

Marine Special Operations Company (Reinforced) Regionalization

The 1st Marine Raider Battalion and 1st Marine Raider Support Battalion are oriented toward supporting United States Pacific Command. The 2d Marine Raider Battalion and 2d Marine Raider Support Battalion are oriented toward supporting United States Central Command. The 3d Marine Raider Battalion and 3d Marine Raider Support Battalion are oriented toward supporting United States Africa Command. These different regional orientations each produce slight differences in equipping, operational requirements and TTP within each MSOC (rein). For example, a MSOC (rein) deploying in support of United States Pacific Command (formed from 1st Marine Raider Battalion and 1st Marine Raider Support Battalion) devotes training to developing additional maritime skills and capabilities required by their region; their individual and unit equipment requirements are also altered to support that requirement. The MSOC (rein) can readily alter their training focus or task organization to produce theater-specific capabilities when directed by the priorities of the GCC, CDRTSOC, or COMMARFORSOC.

Similar differences can be seen in the inherent foreign language capabilities of the MSOC (rein). The core languages for the Marines of 1st Marine Raider Battalion are Tagalog and Indonesian, while the core language for the Marines of 2d Marine Raider Battalion is Modern Standard Arabic. The core languages for the Marines of 3d Marine Raider Battalion are French and Modern Standard Arabic. Other languages are taught on an as-needed basis. In addition to core language instruction, each battalion provides theater-specific cultural instruction throughout their predeployment training program.

CHAPTER 6
MARINE FORCES SPECIAL
OPERATIONS COMMAND LOGISTICS

The joint character of special operations necessitates support arrangements across the Services, with emphasis on unique support required to sustain independent and widely distributed operations. Marine Forces Special Operations Command works in coordination with the TSOC to ensure appropriate MARSOF are provided to meet operational requirements outlined by the respective GCC. The GCCs and their Service component commanders (e.g., MARFOR commands), in coordination with the TSOC, are responsible for ensuring effective and responsive systems are developed and provided for supporting assigned or attached SOF in their area of operation.

Logistic support for MARFORSOC is the responsibility of Marine Corps Logistics Command C2 structure, except where otherwise provided for by support agreements or other directives. This support is executed via the theater MARFOR in coordination with the supported TSOC. This responsibility exists regardless of whether the MARFORSOC unit requiring support is assigned to the Service component, the TSOC, or a specific JTF.

The CDRUSSOCOM is responsible for developing and acquiring special operations-peculiar equipment, materials, supplies, and services. This support will be provided to theater-deployed SOF via USSOCOM Service component logistic infrastructures and in conjunction with theater Service components.

Unless stated otherwise, the TSOC is the supported commander for deployed MARSOF. The TSOC will coordinate common-item logistic support with theater MARFORs based on requirements submitted in the MARSOF statement of requirements (SORs). The TSOC coordinates with the GCC for support that neither it nor the theater MARFOR can meet and publishes a concept of logistic support for the deploying MARSOF. The theater MARFOR is the supporting unit and will coordinate with HQMC to resolve logistic issues that cannot be solved at the component level. Theater MARFORs coordinate common-user logistic support with TSOCs and provide support options and limitations. Additionally, theater MARFORs—

- Provide and/or coordinate Service-common logistic support and inform the GCC of plans or changes in logistic support that would significantly affect operational capability or sustainability.
- Plan, coordinate, and execute support for special technical operations conducted by, or in support of, Marine Corps forces through the GCC.
- Identify and coordinate required Marine Corps logistic support at the operational-level.
- Organize logistic support throughout the GCCs AOR.

- Develop agreements with other Service component commanders.
- Participate in component command-level working groups.

Deployed MSOCs possess a very limited tactical-level organic logistic capability through assignment of CSS personnel from the following logistic functional areas: aerial delivery, embarkation, engineer, landing support, maintenance, motor transport, parachute rigger, and supply. The LST tasked to support the MSOC is intended to be collocated with the TSOC and perform operational-level logistic functional area coordination with the TSOC, theater MARFOR, and other theater support agencies.

The unique composition and distributed employment of SOF presents the supported GCC with challenges in tailoring the operational-level theater support network resources to provide tactical-level logistic support and sustainment. Special operations forces are designed with lean logistic capabilities and are dependent upon geographic combatant command theater support network resources for CSS and sustainment. The MARSOF is capable of sustainment for an initial 15-day period, but are dependent upon theater resources in all logistic functional areas beyond that initial entry period and dependent upon theater resources for all CSS. The MARSOF commanders must submit comprehensive logistic support and sustainment requirements to TSOCs and theater MARFORs via a SOR that provides mission analysis and a detailed equipment density list.

STATEMENT OF REQUIREMENTS

The COMMARFORSOC submits an initial SOR message to the appropriate TSOC no later than 180-days from deployment, with a concurrent notification to the appropriate theater MARFOR. A second, refined SOR is submitted no later than 90 days from deployment containing any changes or refinements. Each SOR message requests TSOC coordination with the theater MARFOR and GCC concerning the development of a concept of logistic support for MARSOF. Subsequent SOR messages may be submitted as required prior to deployment to confirm or change support requirements.

The SOR will identify the sustainment requirements as Service-common or special operations-peculiar. Service-common items include standard military items, base operating support, and the supplies and services provided by the Marine Corps to support and sustain its own forces, including those assigned to the combatant commands. Items and services defined as Service-common by one Service are not necessarily Service-common for all other Services. The majority of MARSOF equipment is Marine Corps Service-common. Special operations-peculiar equipment is that material, supplies, and services required for special operations for which there is not a Service-common requirement.

The MARFORSOC CSS personnel are required to become proficient in areas beyond their primary MOS training. The MARSOF logistic requirements necessitate cross-functional and cross-Service operations. This includes the use of applicable logistic information systems necessary to access the theater support network. Each theater support network may use different Service systems, but all MARSOF deployments include personnel proficient in the use of the following systems:

- Global Combat Service Support System–Marine Corps.
- USSOCOM's Special Operations Forces Sustainment, Asset Visibility, and Information Exchange.
- Marine Corps Common Logistics Command and Control System.
- US Army's Property Book Unit Supply Enhanced systems.

TYPICAL DEPLOYED MARINE SPECIAL OPERATIONS FORCES SUSTAINMENT

Combat service support requirements are identified and coordinated through the supported TSOC.

The MARSOF will identify requirements for all classes of supply beyond the initial 15 days and rely upon the geographic combatant command theater support network as identified/coordinated by the TSOC concept of logistics support.

The MARSOF deploys with limited field maintenance capabilities. Secondary reparable and maintenance support above organic capability will be identified for coordination between the theater MARFOR (Service-common) and TSOC (special operations-peculiar).

The MARSOF deploys via inter-theater air and surface lifts, but is mission postured through intra-theater air and surface lifts. Both inter- and intra-theater lifts will be scheduled and coordinated via the time-phased force and deployment data process with and by the supported TSOC. Additionally, MARSOF relies on the TSOC and theater enablers to support its port handling/in-land transportation requirements. Lifts of opportunity, such as other Service air and surface craft, will be coordinated as needed and synchronized through the TSOC.

The MARSOF deploys with limited tactical wheeled vehicles, nonstandard tactical vehicles, and materials handling equipment. The MARSOF requirements for garrison mobile equipment, such as pick-up trucks, stake-bed trucks, and buses, are identified during mission analysis. The MARSOF deploys with limited engineer support capabilities, support requirements beyond organic capability will be identified to the TSOC and MARFOR.

The MARSOF deploys with a limited HSS capability (independent duty corpsman and corpsmen). The MARSOF HSS requirements beyond organic capability, to include access to higher, adjacent, and supporting HSS capability and facilities, will be identified to the TSOC and MARFOR.

The MARSOF deploys with a very limited organic services capability. Services support such as morale, welfare, and recreation; postal; disbursing; and access to religious activities will be identified to the TSOC and MARFOR.

The MARSOF may deploy with a limited contingency contracting capability. The MARSOF commanders have a working knowledge of contingency contracting and designate appropriate personnel to establish, maintain, and ensure the payment of local contracts, to include designation and training of a field-ordering officer to establish and/or monitor contracts as a contracting officer's representative and a paying agent to disburse the funds, including operational funds. Contracting requirements beyond organic capabilities/authorities will be identified to the TSOC and MARFOR.

CHAPTER 7
MARINE FORCES SPECIAL OPERATIONS COMMAND TRAINING AND EDUCATION

TRAINING AND EDUCATION PHILOSOPHY

Marine Forces Special Operations Command's training and education philosophy is as follows:

- Invest in training and education to sustain the current fight and increase knowledge and skills for the future fight.
- Understand and think critically about the global environment.
- Link training to tasks relative to future areas of operation, and utilize the time-tested systems approach to training.
- Employ processes that create a unique blend of capabilities that drive the training and education vision to prepare and empower MARSOF to operate in austere and complex political environments against ever-adapting enemies.

TRAINING PRINCIPLES

The MARFORSOC training and education system is germane to all required mission areas, training events, and readiness assessments. This system can be applied to prepare Marines across the range of military operations, levels of war, and all operational phases. For these reasons, every MARFORSOC leader must understand the command's training system and ensure their respective organizations' training programs support the accomplishment of COMMARFORSOC training objectives.

Effective training is the key to achieving maximum readiness for the performance of all SOF missions. The MARFORSOC training system provides the policy and processes for developing personnel; it includes individual training, leader training, unit training, joint/combined training, and training support.

Marine Forces Special Operations Command has established a process that sustains the framework of the component training system. Commander's guidance sets the training principles which focus the effort of resources in order to feed a training cycle that covers the initial, individual, collective, advanced, sustainment, and predeployment training requirements. The training cycle results in individual and unit operational capability for global employment.

The MARFORSOC training methodology is guided by the following principles:

- Commanders are responsible for all training.
- Maintain mission focus.
- Conduct detailed planning with decentralized execution.
- Prioritize for efficiency.
- Balance individual and collective training.
- Evaluate and seek continuous process improvement.
- Conduct rigorous training assessment.
- Train to perform seamlessly at the tactical, operational, and strategic level—the "three chess boards" training and education methodology (see fig. 7-1).
- Maximize the use of modeling and simulation.
- Train during deployment.
- Apply joint and USSOCOM TTP and lessons learned.
- Foster a learning organization.
- Ensure SOF interoperability.

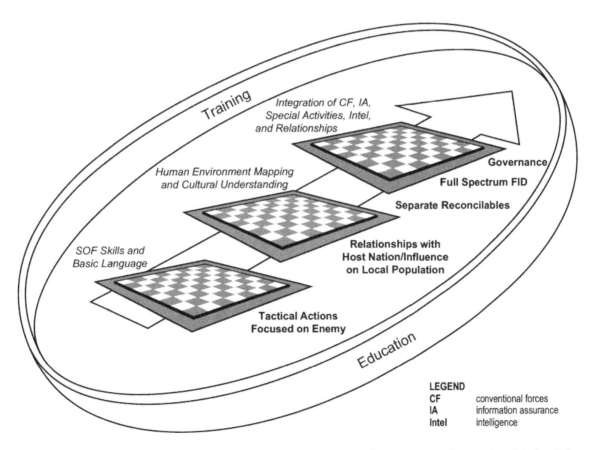

Figure 7-1. Marine Forces Special Operations Command Training and Education Methodology.

INDIVIDUAL AND COLLECTIVE TRAINING SYNERGY

One of MARFORSOC's unique attributes is the ability to rapidly task-organize an appropriately scaled and integrated special operations force and deploy it to conduct enabled, distributed operations across remote, austere, and ambiguous environments. The key to this force generation is the ability to refine the individual SOO/CSO capabilities through advanced individual and collective training (guided by training principles and processes), bringing all those capabilities together well in advance of deployment.

For all MARSOF, individual skills are developed through introductory training schools and through follow-on courses during the individual training phase prior to deployment. Once the force is task-organized and brought together for collective training, the force develops its integrated capabilities during the unit training phase.

SPECIAL OPERATIONS CAREER PROGRESSION METHODOLOGY

The MARFORSOC skills are a collection of standardized capabilities and training, both collective and individual that must be sustained in order to support all the warfighting functions and activities required to execute the special operations. These skills are under constant evaluation and updated in order to maintain the capability to execute missions in the ever-changing complex combination of political, technical, and topographical environments.

The career progression for a SOO and CSO are managed in order to meet the requirements of both the Service and the component.

SPECIAL OPERATIONS CAPABILITY
SPECIALIST AND COMBAT SERVICE SUPPORT TRAINING

Task organization is inherent in all MARSOF operations. Tailored combat support, CSS, and other specialized capabilities are intrinsic to MARSOF and make the deployable units capable of sustainable expeditionary operations in the most austere environments. Task organization in MARFORSOC is driven by operational requirements and can include intelligence personnel, MPCs, EOD, JTAC, specialized communications capability, and/or CSS (e.g., personnel administration, embarkation, motor transport, air delivery, maintenance, general engineering, supply).

The SOCSs complete specialized training in the individual training phase prior to task-organizing as part of an MSOT, MSOC, or SOTF. In order to be designated fully trained, SOCS must complete the Special Operations Training Course; full-spectrum SERE training; and the appropriate SOF training for their MOS. The Special Operations Training Course is designed to train all SOCSs in the warfighting skills necessary to "shoot, move, and communicate" as an integral component of their assigned MARSOF unit in the distributed environment. Table 7-1 details the SOF-specific training MARFORSOC provides to produce the required SOCS capability. Combat service support Marines may also attend SOF training based upon space available and mission support requirements.

Table 7-1. Special Operations Capability Specialist Training.

	Marine Corps Training	SOF Training
Intelligence	Service entry training MOS school Pre-deployment Training Program, blocks III & IV MOS experience	SOF training course Tactical Combat Casualty Care Full-spectrum SERE Multidiscipline Intelligence Operators Course Operations/Intelligence Integration Course Collective SOF intelligence training
EOD	Service entry training MOS school Pre-deployment Training Program, blocks III & IV MOS experience	SOF training course Tactical Combat Casualty Care Full-spectrum SERE SOF EOD, levels I & II USSOCOM Sensitive Site Exploitation/Biometric Marine Technical Surveillance Course Insertion Capability
MPC	Service entry training MOS school Military Working Dog Course Pre-deployment Training Program, blocks III & IV MOS experience	SOF training course Tactical Combat Casualty Care Full-spectrum SERE Basic MPC Handler Course Advanced MPC Handler Course
JTAC	Service entry training MOS school Marine Artillery Scout Observer Course Pre-deployment Training Program, blocks III & IV MOS experience	SOF training course Tactical Combat Casualty Care Full-spectrum SERE Airborne/Multimission Parachute Course Battle Damage Assessment Fire Support Chiefs Course
Communications	Service entry training MOS school Pre-deployment Training Program, blocks III & IV MOS experience	SOF training course Tactical Combat Casualty Care Full-spectrum SERE MARSOC Network Operators Course/MSOT systems Advanced Network Operators Course/MSOC systems Enterprise Network Operators Course/SOTF systems

UNIT TRAINING PHASE

The unit training phase is a combination of standard training events and specific training requirements as derived from a detailed mission analysis for the upcoming deployment. This mission analysis also drives the capability types and total number of personnel necessary to accomplish each specific task. These enabling capabilities are fully integrated into all aspects of the deploying unit's predeployment training program, resulting in a fully functional and cohesive team, enabled for sustained expeditionary operations.

Figure 7-2 depicts a standard predeployment training cycle for an MSOC to develop an integrated force package. Enabling capabilities are identified and prepared approximately 6 months prior to transfer of authority in-theater. The identified enabling capabilities are attached to the deploying unit and fully integrated into the team and company collective training phases. This phase creates cohesion and ensures that these enabling capabilities are holistically integrated throughout training. The full capability of the deploying MARSOF unit is created, trained, and certified through this unit training phase process.

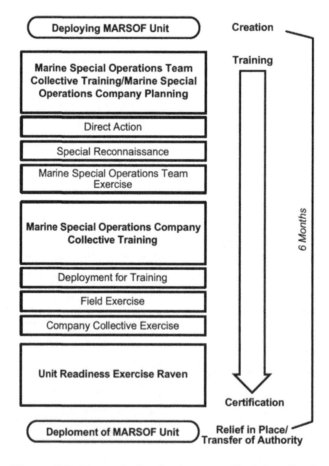

Figure 7-2. Example Predeployment Training Cycle.

EDUCATION

Educational opportunities must be encouraged, valued, and promoted. Attendance at advanced educational programs should be viewed favorably for purposes of evaluations, developmental selections, and promotions. Marine Forces Special Operations Command will further develop educational opportunities for all assigned Service members such as executive-level seminars or programs that provide academic certificates. Marine Forces Special Operations Command will manage the baseline educational requirements along four lines of effort: post-secondary education, foreign language education, regional studies, and professional military education (PME).

Critical skills operators and SOCS are the backbone of MARFORSOC, and they will be the core of the education philosophy. They focus on educational opportunities early in their careers and they appreciate that professional education is continuous and will enhance their ability to craft innovative solutions to complex problems.

Professional military education is rounded by a reading program that recommends diverse topics that support the command and individual areas of expertise. All MARFORSOC members are encouraged to participate in all reading programs available, to include, but not limited to, the following:

- Marine Corps Commandant's Professional Reading List.
- USSOCOM Commander's Reading List.
- TSOC Recommended Reading.

Marine Forces Special Operations Command will continuously evaluate and expand educational opportunities along the four lines of effort identified by USSOCOM and the Marine Corps: post-secondary education, foreign language education, regional studies, and PME.

Post-Secondary Education

The MARSOC places emphasis on the following post-secondary education opportunities that benefit both the organization and the individual:

- Opportunities for enlisted personnel to obtain college credit from SOF MOS schools that can be applied toward an associate's or bachelor's degree should be maximized.
- Marine Forces Special Operations Command enlisted personnel and warrant officers will be provided opportunities and support to earn a bachelor's degree by the grade of E-8/E-9 and CWO-3/CWO-4. Marine Forces Special Operations Command will facilitate this through academic counseling, talent development, and increased educational opportunities.
- The MARFORSOC officers are encouraged to earn a master's degree in a relevant area of study by the grade of O-5. Numerous programs are available, to include traditional Service programs, civilian institutions, and planned Joint Special Operations University-sponsored programs.

- Programs within Naval Post Graduate School's Department of Defense Analysis Department are the cornerstone of SOF advanced education, and Service schools are the foundation of our force's development.
- The MARFORSOC civilian personnel will maximize available career programs. The plan will leverage Service PME, advanced academic degree programs, and Office of Personnel Management leadership development programs. The focus areas will build competencies that are the foundation for outstanding leadership and management performance.

Foreign Language Education

Language skills are central to SOF's ability to establish credibility, build rapport, maintain situational awareness, and effectively communicate with foreign partners. Collective and individual language capabilities are a significant investment in individual intellectual capital and unit training time. Marine Forces Special Operations Command continues to develop and sustain language capability in the identified languages. Language proficiency is supported with detailed cultural education specific to the region of interest. The balance of language and cultural awareness is critical to operational competency. Additional information regarding foreign language training and employment can be found in chapter 4, related to the MSOS BLCs, and chapter 5, related to the MSOC (rein) regionalization.

Regional Studies

Regional knowledge is a critical capability in special operations. The investment in regional proficiency must be made years in advance of crisis response. The next crisis area cannot be predicted, but through strategic studies and analysis, areas of concern can be monitored; in some cases through dedicated operations a crisis may be prevented. Regional studies must be holistic in nature and include concentrations in diplomacy, ideology, military, and economics (commonly referred to as DIME). Personnel newly assigned to MARFORSOC will complete Service, or an equivalent, basic cross-cultural competency instruction. Marine special operations forces working with foreign partners, allies, or coalition forces will complete Service, or an equivalent, predeployment region-specific instruction.

Professional Military Education

Participation in PME is an institutional expectation. The MARFORSOC must invest in the long-term development of the force by ensuring Service members are provided the opportunity to complete their required Service and SOF PME programs by balancing operational tempo with educational opportunities.

Marine Forces Special Operations Command members will be encouraged to attend graduate-level, intermediate, and senior PME. The MARFORSOC will inform SOF PME attendees of the command's expectation that they enroll in SOF electives and pursue research topics valuable to special operations.

Both commands and Service members accept the responsibility that Service PME requirements are required as a foundational education opportunity. Marine Forces Special Operations Command members are encouraged to complete the PME minimum requirements, but also establish and grow relationships with the Marine Corps University and the Gray Research Center or Service equivalent in order to participate in those education and research initiatives that support both the USMC and SOF research areas. The professional dialogue between MARFORSOC members of all ranks with conventional force counterparts in the educational setting will reinforce operational collaboration initiatives.

CHAPTER 8
MARINE FORCES SPECIAL OPERATIONS COMMAND AND MARINE AIR-GROUND TASK FORCE INTEROPERABILITY AND INTERDEPENDENCE

As a MAGTF forms and prepares to deploy, the opportunities for MAGTF and SOF interoperability are numerous. This provides a force option unmatched in quality and capability in today's complex operating environment. This level of interoperability between two elements possessing Marine common bonds facilitates multiple benefits in support of Service and SOF operations.

The Marine Corps and MARFORSOC relationship, strengthened with collaboration and interoperability through Title 10 war games and large-scale exercises, creates a force option capable of rapid deployment and sustained presence. This mutually supporting relationship creates operational latitude and depth in capability, while demonstrating resource efficiency through continued collaboration in SOF and service concepts, systems, and equipment. Annual participation in war games and exercises strengthens the bond and demonstrates the interoperability of the MAGTF and SOF. Additionally, collaboration in science and technology keeps both the Service and SOF on the leading edge of technology and weaponry procurement. This operational synergy is designed to produce rapid effects across the range of military operations in all environments blending *"Any Clime and Place"* and *"Always Forward."*

Marine Forces Special Operations Command has the capability to produce positive effects towards achieving the Nation's objectives when used correctly, as with all USSOCOM components, in coordination with the conventional force. Marine Forces Special Operations Command will apply a combination of direct and indirect approaches during the operational phases.

The operational phases 0 through V in figure 8-1, on page 8-2, correlate to the type of approach (direct or indirect) and activity that should be considered when planning for conventional forces: SOF type integration, interoperability, and interdependence.

Special operations force enabling activities in Phase 0
- Building partner capacity: security forces for later actions
- Information exchange: situational awareness during "approach"
- Preparation of the environment: establishing networks

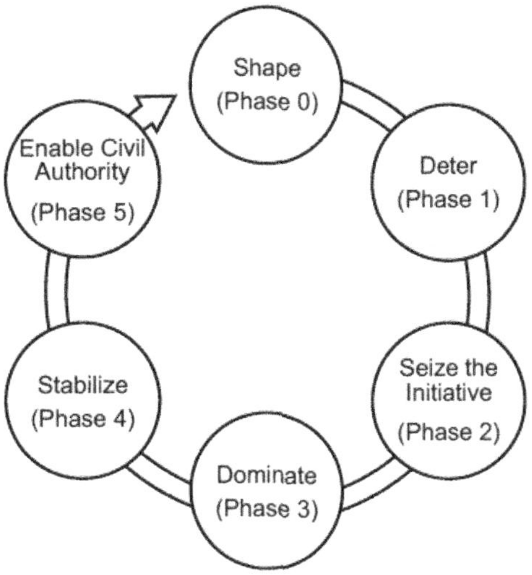

Mutually supporting activities in Phases 2–5
- Preparation of the environment/unconventional warfare: Activate network for arrival of MAGTF
- Special reconnaissance: Provide up to date intelligence
- Direct action: Actions to reduce threat in area of operation

Special operations force actions by phase	
0	• Building partner capacity • Preparation of the environment • Information exchange exercises • Joint combined exchange training
1	• Special reconnaissance • Unconventional warfare • Security force assistance • Preparation of the environment • Direct action
2	• Direct action • Special reconnaissance • Unconventional warfare
3	• Direct action • Special reconnaissance • Unconventional warfare
4	• Counterinsurgency • Foreign internal defense • Security force assistance
5	• Security force assistance • Foreign internal defense • Civil affairs

Phases: Shape (Phase 0), Deter (Phase 1), Seize the Initiative (Phase 2), Dominate (Phase 3), Stabilize (Phase 4), Enable Civil Authority (Phase 5)

Figure 8-1. Concept of SOF and MAGTF Interoperability by Operational Phase.

CONCEPTS AND PROGRAMS INTEGRATION

Posturing the force to meet the defense challenges of today and the future, the Marine Corps and MARFORSOC conduct professional and information exchanges through wargaming, exercises, and experimentation. Today's operating environment demands close integration of conventional forces, special operations, interagency, and multinational partners conducting the full range of military operations. Forward-deployed MAGTFs and MARSOF, operating within the same region, provide increased opportunity for interoperability between the Marine Corps and the special operations community (see fig. 8-2 on page 8-3). Sharing common bonds, each force provides dynamic effects by projecting their individual characters and capabilities of expeditionary and special operations in support of the national security strategy.

The seamless transition from concepts to forward-deployed operational relationships will progress through the following planned initiatives (see app. A for assessment criteria):

- Deliberate and early integration of SOF planners in major Marine Corps exercises.
- Deliberate and early integration of SOF planners in Service war games.

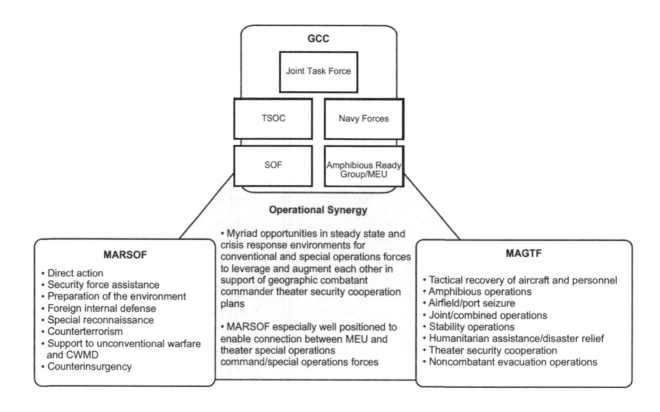

Figure 8-2. Example of MAGTF and MARSOF Areas of Integration and Interoperability.

- Development of limited objective experiments focused on operational and capabilities integration in complex terrain and circumstances that explore relationships, information sharing, and equipment interoperability.
- Deliberate planning opportunities among the regional MARFOR, Navy forces, and TSOC for security cooperation events.

The ability to build partner nation capacity while maintaining US interests abroad requires a comprehensive approach with a force that possesses the capability and depth to develop and sustain relationships in the region. As conventional Marine Corps forces and MARSOF continue to communicate, the integration process will mature and achieve tangible results.

CRISIS RESPONSE

The national security strategy requires a rapid response to crisis, capable of protecting national interests and preserving lives. This makes the MAGTF and SOF a viable option, providing force and flexibility. The blend of expeditionary ethos, rapid planning processes, relevant regional knowledge, interagency relationships, and organic warfighting capability across the range of military operations provides an unmatched degree of readiness. In uncertain situations, the knowledge that a composite force can rapidly deploy and provide immediate effects provides the GCC a level of capability and confidence knowing that the initial response is appropriate and flexible. While providing immediate action, the continuous process of assessments is conducted in order to report the current situation with recommendations for follow-on actions during all phases. This demonstrates the synergy of the MAGTF and SOF. A forward-deployed SOF, with an established footprint, communicates the evolving situation to the MAGTF, which provides a sustained national response.

SPECIAL OPERATIONS FORCES LIAISON ELEMENT

The amphibious ready group/MEU special operations forces liaison element (SOFLE) is a USSOCOM concept to enhance coordination and liaison between SOF and the amphibious ready group/MEU, with a joint SOF element. The SOFLE provides the critical links to the SOF network, the TSOC forward-deployed SOF elements, and interagency partners.

The SOFLE consists of experienced SOF personnel from across USSOCOM. These personnel provide experienced SOF leadership as well as specific capability in the form of intelligence analysis, communications, and liaison to the TSOC (see fig. 8-3 on page 8-5). The SOFLE supports the conventional force starting with the early stages of predeployment training and operationally throughout the deployment. Utilizing SOF-unique communications networks, the SOFLE provides current and real-time information from the SOF network to the supported commander in order to leverage and employ each other's capabilities, forces, strengths, and advantages to provide and achieve greater mutual operational support and synergy in servicing GCC objectives.

As the Marine Corps and MARFORSOC continue to deploy globally it is certain they will operate in many of the same complex and uncertain environments. Collaboration between SOF and Services will facilitate cross-organizational knowledge and communication for dynamic responses to rapidly evolving events.

0-5	E-6	E-7
SOFLE LDR	**SOFLE INTEL ANALYST**	**SOFLE COMMS SNCO**
SOF leader w/theater SOF OAA experience	SOF enabler with experience at the tactical and or operational level	Senior SOF enabler with experience at the tactical and or operational level
Capable of advising on tactical level SOF-MEU/ARG combined operations	Capable of performing all source analysis using SOF IO/TTP	Capable of operating relevant SOF and common service C4I

E-8	E-5	E-5
SOFLE ASST LDR	**SOFLE COMMS OPERATOR**	**SOFLE COMMS OPERATOR**
SOF leader w/theater SOF OAA experience	SOF enabler with experience at the tactical and or operational level	SOF enabler with experience at the tactical and or operational level
Capable of advising on tactical level SOF-MEU/ARG combined operations	Capable of operating relevant SOF and common service C4I	Capable of operating relevant SOFand common service C4I

+ | MEU LNO to TSOC |

LEGEND

ARG	amphibious ready group
ASST	assistant
COMMS	communications
IO	intelligence operations
LDR	leader
LNO	liaison officer
MEU	Marine expeditionary unit
OAA	operations, activities, and actions
SNCO	staff noncommissioned officer
SOFLE	speical operations forces liaison element
TSOC	theater special operations command

Figure 8-3. Example of Special Operations Forces Liaison Element Organization.

This Page Intentionally Left Blank

CHAPTER 9
MARINE FORCES
SPECIAL OPERATIONS COMMAND
PRESERVATION OF THE FORCE AND FAMILY

The MPOTFF includes six pillars: human performance, spiritual performance, family readiness, HSS, safety, and transition. Each pillar can operate independently, but is more effective when integrated and synchronized. The purpose of MPOTFF is to provide a one-stop shop for the MARFORSOC family to provide resourcing and assistance in the six pillars that make up MPOTFF. This assistance begins when a Marine, Sailor, and family enter MARFORSOC and continues through transition and onto a successful journey in life after MARFORSOC. Even though Marines, Sailors, and their families will leave MARFORSOC, they will always be "MARFORSOC for Life."

In addition, MPOTFF develops a culture that supports our leaders in developing, training, and educating personnel to achieve and maintain physical, mental, spiritual, and family excellence that will better enable them to meet challenges during their MARFORSOC career.

DESIGN

The MPOTFF initiative is developing an organizational culture that exemplifies and supports performance and resilience throughout the command. For any individual, the achievement of this goal rests on four foundational concepts that together constitute the whole person. They are *body–mind–spirit–family*. These four components support personal performance in all individuals whether they are Marines, family members, civilian employees, or contractors. In order to serve as a basis for exceptional performance and personal resilience, all four components must be firmly established, balanced, and focused on excellence. This foundation of *body–mind–spirit–family* will provide the balance and internal strength required to sustain honorable character, high performance, and resiliency under continuous, high demand conditions.

Marine Corps values and the SOF truths all focus on people as the most important element in the SOF capability equation and the MPOTFF. Marine Corps values—honor, courage, commitment—all focus on the attributes that make Marines and Sailors effective. The SOF truths emphasize that the quality of our people involved is mission critical—and that groups of quality people cannot be mass-produced or produced on short notice. In combination, spiritual, mental, and physical strengths make our Marines and Sailors not only more mission effective, but also ultimately more effective in their family, social, and career lives.

Marine Forces Special Operation Command's devotion to its people via MPOTFF will be executed across the command and throughout its community. The initial priority of effort will be on MARFORSOC's uniformed personnel. This phase will include tailoring the policies, manpower, facilities, and equipment to support physical, psychological, and spiritual needs; transition to civilian life; force preservation; and social well-being. The second priority of effort is taking care of its family members, with the understanding that our Marines cannot be mission-ready if they are not prepared at home. This phase will utilize MPOTFF social performance, HQMC Family Readiness, and Marine Corps Community Services support to increase the number of personnel and programs required for the uniqueness of the MARFORSOC family.

The implementation of Human Performance and Resiliency Centers within the command fills a SOF-specific need that allows speedy access to embedded subject matter expertise. These organic, trusted agents provide a continuum of warfighter performance from pro-habilitative strengthening and training to rehabilitative and clinical care, extending the careers and enhancing the quality of life of highly-trained MARFORSOC Marines, Sailors, and their family members. The management and maintenance of these centers and the associated equipment will be critical to the success of the program and developing the organizational culture of MPOTFF within MARFORSOC.

Figure 9-1, on page 9-3, gives the conceptual depiction of the culture, which is MARFORSOC's holistic, integrated approach to the MPOTFF. The MPOTFF construct is designed to provide tools to help improvise and adapt, as well as reinforce core beliefs and values. This construct is oriented along the *body–mind–spirit–family* lines of effort. These foundational areas of personal development and excellence reinforce building connections, enhancing communications, optimizing performance and resilience, increasing a sense of community, and strengthening commitments.

ORGANIZATION

United States Special Operations Command and MARFORSOC surveys have indicated that one of the problems with current support programs is that Service members and their families are not comfortable requesting help from people they do not know. A solution is to provide embedded, organic support assets into the operational units. This allows a relationship to be formed between the support personnel (trusted agents) and the Marines, Sailors, and their families. The organization of existing support personnel, such as physical therapists, chaplains, mental health professionals, and family readiness officers should be reviewed to determine if re-alignment into units and/or additional unit positions could provide greater benefits to the command.

Headquarters MARFORSOC maximizes sourcing requirements at the component level and is coordinated through the MPOTFF lead. Major subordinate commands (regiment, support group, school) will avoid centralizing MPOTFF assets, and instead push them to embed in units. While centralization can be more efficient from a support perspective, in some cases, it limits effectiveness.

**Figure 9-1. Marine Forces Special Operations Command
Preservation of the Force and Family Focus Area Relationships.**

The baseline of personnel in MARFORSOC that currently fills MPOTFF-related positions will be comprised of the following personnel: psychologists, chaplains, physical therapists, military and family life consultants, and strength/conditioning and athletic trainers. Manpower will first be filled with contractors and, in a limited role, with military and civilian positions. This strategy serves a two-fold purpose: it allows hard-to-fill positions (e.g., operational psychologist) to be filled sooner and allows flexibility in tailoring the positions. As the MPOTFF initiative matures, an analysis conducted at periodic intervals will help determine any excesses or gaps in the staffing provided. Contractor manpower will be adjusted accordingly. The intent is for the contracts to be maintained until the position can be converted and successfully filled as a military or civilian position, or it is deemed unnecessary.

The organization of the MPOTFF program is led by the MPOTFF director, who is a member of the special staff. The MPOTFF is also augmented by a special amphibious reconnaissance corpsmen, Marine Corps Community Services, and Care Coalition representatives, thus increasing capability.

In addition, MPOTFF develops a culture that supports our leaders in developing, training, and educating personnel to achieve and maintain physical, mental, spiritual, and family excellence that will better enable them to meet challenges during their MARFORSOC career.

TRAINING AND OBJECTIVES

Multiple aspects of training are utilized to enhance the performance and resiliency of MARFORSOC forces. All MPOTFF staff actively supports the culture through two distinct components: performance training (training/operations or pro-habilitative support) or rehabilitation and/or clinical care (healthcare screening and treatment or rehabilitative support). In their role supporting performance and resiliency training, the staff's focus is on the provision of intrapersonal (centered in the individual) and interpersonal (interacting with others) tactics, training methods, and strategic processes to enhance performance and improve focus on achievement of mission-related objectives. These efforts can be focused at the individual, team, or larger organizational level. In their role supporting the rehabilitation and clinical care function, the MPOTFF staff's focus is on detection and remediation of impediments to Service and family member capability, stability, or motivation.

Performance coaching, individual and group instruction, resiliency education, and rehabilitative and clinical care are examples of primary models for performance and resiliency development and therapeutic services that can be delivered organically within the command. Supplemental educational opportunities and services for the Service member and their families are also available through HQMC and Marine Corps Community Services. This symbiotic relationship further reinforces the fifth SOF truth "Most special operations require non-SOF support."

Training opportunities will be examined and their feasibility will be continuously evaluated. Opportunities to apply training and education resources will be developed for the member, spouse, and family. The training breaks down into medical, human performance, behavioral health, spiritual performance, family readiness, force preservation, and transition.

PILLAR DESCRIPTIONS

The MPOTFF concept includes embedding support in units to build rapport with individual members and their families in order to proactively resolve issues and provide tools and strategies for anticipated stressors. This methodology encourages the MARFORSOC unit member to reach out to the embedded faculty member as opposed to current DOD methodology, which centrally manages sources and relies on pushing education and updates to the Service member. This will be accomplished, in part, through embedding key support infrastructure in each unit to build trust and increase mutual commitment. This concept will complement existing support services.

Medical/Health Service Support

The mission of MARFORSOC medical is to globally deliver leading edge health services to our Service members through agile, patient-centered care. Health service support trains, develops, and equips a multidisciplinary medical force that supports full-spectrum special operations. This multidisciplinary team and Marine-Centered Medical Home model provides a multitude of capabilities to include primary care, undersea medicine, dental, case management, referral assistance, limited duty coordination, medical planning and logistics, and environmental health, among other specialties.

Behavioral Health
The MARFORSOC behavioral health team consists of clinical psychologists, licensed clinical social workers, and military and family life consultants assigned to focus on the clinical care of behavioral health issues and stress-related problems affecting individual members and families. These professionals have clinical experience in medical settings and are licensed and credentialed by the appropriate professional agencies.

Human Performance
The Human Performance Program provides staff, facilities, and equipment to support the long-term performance and health of MARFORSOC personnel and, when available, families. The staff includes physical therapists, athletic trainers, strength and conditioning specialists, sports psychologists, and dietitians focused on improving physical and cognitive performance and resilience. They aim to provide proven strength and conditioning and sports psychology methods to minimize future injury and maximize physical and cognitive performance, enhancing stress mitigation and critical decision-making skill sets of personnel and family members. The embedded human performance therapy team is focused on accelerating the safe return from an injury back to deployment or training, and the dietitian provides education and guidance on performance nutrition to optimize the effects of the diet fueling the warrior.

Spiritual Performance
Spiritual performance is supported by the MARFORSOC religious ministry team. The religious ministry team supports the holistic development and care of Marines, Sailors, and their family members through the full complement of religious programs. The chaplains guide people to better understand themselves and seek self-improvement through classroom presentations, religious functions, counseling, coaching, and resource sharing. Chaplains strengthen the chain of command and assist in the development of leadership by providing advice to leaders at all levels. The end state of the MPOTFF spiritual support is to develop mission-ready Marines, Sailors and their families, who demonstrate spiritual, moral, and ethical maturity supported by the innovative delivery of religious ministry and compassionate pastoral care. Mission-ready Marines and Sailors are spiritually resilient people who use values to make decisions and put those decisions into action in daily life. They have the ability to engage in healthy relationships with people and with an individual's beliefs or philosophies, and they have the ability to make meaning out of life's events.

Family Readiness
Marine Forces Special Operations Command's family readiness team has successfully shifted from the traditional Marine Corps focus of primary support to the Marine and Sailor, to educating and resourcing family members first, allowing them to support themselves through personal growth and development of their own mind, body, and spirit that can then carry over to the Service member. This paradigm shift has restructured resources, messaging, and language within family readiness to mirror the performance and resiliency (commonly referred to as PERRES) mission so that a Service member and spouse and/or family member are consistent in their performance and resilience at home.

Force Preservation/Safety

Force preservation is a vital element of MARFORSOC's combat readiness; death, serious injury, and the loss of material assets due to mishaps directly and negatively impacts the warfighting capability of the entire command. Marine Forces Special Operations Command recognizes that engaged leadership at all levels is the key to ensuring a command climate that demands the preservation of our Marines and their family member's assets through risk management. Marine Forces Special Operations Command has established and maintains a vibrant and viable force preservation and safety program where maintaining combat readiness, eliminating preventable mishaps, and preserving our most precious assets—our Marines, Sailors, family members, civilian personnel, and equipment—is every Marine's goal and responsibility.

Transition

The Transition Readiness Program provides Service members and their families a comprehensive set of services to prepare them to reach their goals when they reintegrate into the civilian sector. The Transition Readiness Seminar, which is an event under the program, helps to develop a comprehensive individual transition plan uniquely tailored to each Service members' circumstances and post military goals. The seminar assists transitioning Service members in the areas of goal setting/identification, finance, education, employment, and veterans' benefits. The seminar guides Service members through the process of developing achievable goals by conducting personal assessments and analyzing skills, knowledge, experience, interests, and abilities. The Transition Readiness Seminar identifies actions and activities designed to organize Service member's transition into manageable tasks.

LEADERSHIP AND EDUCATION

The success of the MPOTFF will require leadership at all levels to work toward instilling a cultural change within MARFORSOC units. Leadership can assist in removing the stigma associated with seeking help and direct/encourage participation in human performance programs for the Service member and family. By encouraging integration among the Marines, Sailors, family members, and performance and resiliency professionals, Service members will gain trust and build relationships with MPOTFF support personnel in order to encourage MARFORSOC members to utilize the skills and knowledge these personnel bring to the units. Leadership efforts are key to affecting the cultural change required to address all forms of stigma: personal, public, and institutional.

The MPOTFF success is an enduring effort. Instituting organizational and cultural change will require modified behavior over time. Capturing organizational processes to reinforce MPOTFF principles and creating organizational artifacts representative of MPOTFF values will facilitate institutionalization. Marine Forces Special Operations Command needs to establish MPOTFF as a program of record and protect MPOTFF identified positions, policies, and practices. Also, it will be important to develop contingency plans when units are reorganized, re-missioned, or shut down, so as to capture the need for the facilities, equipment, and personnel.

APPENDIX A
ASSESSMENTS

DEFINING ASSESSMENT

Assessment is the continuous *monitoring* and *evaluation* of the current situation and progress of a program or operation.

Monitoring is the continuous observation of the current situation to identify opportunities for the force, threats to the force, gaps in information, and progress according to the plan or order.

Evaluation is to compare relevant information on the situation or operations against criteria to judge success or progress.

ASSESSMENT AND THE COMMANDER

Assessment answers the commander's questions—

- Are we doing things right?
- Are we doing the right things?
- Where are we?
- What's next, and when?

ASPECTS OF ASSESSMENT

There are four key aspects of assessment—

- Assessment is continuous throughout planning and execution. Assessment precedes, accompanies, and follows all training and operations.
- Assessment occurs at all echelons and levels of war and applies to all aspects of the operation, while considering all elements of the force as well as the warfighting functions (command and control, intelligence, fires, maneuver, logistics, and force protection).

- Assessment focuses on the goals and purpose of the operation. Assessment must always link and ultimately reflect progress toward accomplishing the purpose.
- Assessment orients on the future. Current and past actions are of little value unless they can serve as a basis for future decisions and actions.

Assessment helps the commander identify success or failure, determines the extent to which required conditions have been met for follow-on actions, and recognizes whether a particular end state has been reached. More specifically, assessment should enable the commander to estimate the overall progress of an operation as it unfolds in the operational environment so he/she can make informed decisions for future actions.

ASSESSMENT COMPONENTS

Assessment has three basic components—

- *Goals*: Tasks, objectives, mission, end state.
- *Feedback*: That continuous flow of information about the changing situation that provides us our reality.
- *Process*: A methodology to help the commander, via the staff, determine the difference between two outcomes, the reasons for the difference, and recommendations for change.

TYPES OF ASSESSMENT

Functional Assessment
Functional assessment is assessment by warfighting function: command and control, intelligence, fires, maneuver, logistics, and force protection. Examples of functional assessment include the S-2 tracking threat and environmental changes or the S-4 monitoring the logistic status to prevent or warn of pending culminating points.

Combat Assessment
JP 1-02 defines combat assessment as the determination of the overall effectiveness of force employment during military operations. The combat assessment has three components: battle damage assessment, munitions effectiveness, and re-attack recommendations. Generally, combat assessment is a process well-suited for conventional operations but it can be applied to SOF/ irregular warfare operations if expanded to account for all the activities MARSOF may conduct.

Assessment Process
The commander is the focal point of the assessment process. The top-down guidance initiates the planning effort leading to a plan of action that also serves as a framework for assessment. Through feedback resulting from execution, the commander uses judgment, intuition, and experience to

update the assessment of the situation and then communicates subsequent decisions based on the updated assessment to the staff and subordinate commanders.

Measures of Performance and Effectiveness. Measures of performance (MOPs) and measures of effectiveness (MOEs) can help us make informed decisions by evaluating the performance of our actions (MOP) and the impact of our actions (MOE):

- A MOP assesses friendly actions by measuring task accomplishment. The MOPs help us answer the question, "Are we doing things right?"
- A MOE assesses our impact through changes in system behavior, capability, or operational environment that is tied to the attainment of an end state, achievement of an objective, or creation of an effect. The MOEs help us answer the question, "Are we doing the right things to achieve success?"
- Since the actions we take to accomplish our tasks connect us to the other elements (adversaries, noncombatants, and infrastructure) of the operational environment, we generally need both measures to conduct meaningful assessments. However, extraneous or long lists of MOPs and MOEs are symptoms of an over-engineered assessment process. To be effective, MOPs and MOEs must be observable, relevant, and measurable.

Observable. If the MOEs and MOPs are to help measure progress, then the user has to be able to see them. Criteria such as: "no massed fires from H-2 to H+10" are not good indicators.

Relevant. The MOEs and MOPs should be relevant to the task or goal they are designed to measure and reviewed continuously during execution to ensure that they remain relevant. If a task is modified in planning, then the MOEs and/or MOPs most likely will need adjustment as well. Developing relevant MOPs are rather straightforward, relevant MOEs are more difficult.

Measurable. The MOEs and MOPs require quantitative or qualitative standards. Quantitative standards are preferable as they are usually more objective than qualitative measures.

COMMANDER'S CRITICAL INFORMATION REQUIREMENT

Commander's critical information requirements (CCIRs) are elements of friendly and enemy information the commander identifies as critical to timely decision making. They focus information management and help the commander and staff assess the operational environment. The CCIRs and MOPs/MOEs are directly linked. The CCIRs identify the commander's specific information needs linked to key decisions that only he/she will make. The command's collection effort keys off the CCIRs. The staff should display, track, and update CCIRs throughout planning and execution to ensure continued relevancy. Too many CCIRs, like too many MOPs and MOEs, will hinder the staff's ability to focus on the essential information the commander truly needs while rapidly consuming the available collection assets.

ASSESSMENT ORGANIZATIONS

The operational planning team provides the framework—purpose, mission, end state, tasks, desired effects, conditions, objectives—to subordinates for assessment.

Commanders form an assessment cell in order to focus on demands for detailed information. The commander must determine the focus, composition, and duties of the assessment cell when created. Focus drives cell composition. Typically, the assessment cell includes a cross-section of warfighting function representatives. Cell members should have a broad range of experiences and a solid understanding of the plan so they can recognize the impact of numerous, interrelated activities on the plan. Assessment cell duties include the following:

- Develop criteria for success and track overall progress toward the command's goals.
- Collate, analyze, and synthesize feedback to assess command progress and provide recommendations for change.
- Develop assessment reporting formats and timelines.
- Develop MOEs (enemy focused) and MOPs (friendly focused) per individual functional areas.

ASSESSMENT IN PLANNING

The commander, armed with the situational understanding gained through planning design, sets the stage for assessment with guidance to subordinate commanders and staff. Guidance may include—

- Elements of operational design such as the commander's vision of how he/she sees the operation unfolding, creating the basis for measuring progress.
- Focus areas for assessment.
- CCIRs.

The operational planning team, informed by the commander's planning design, creates a framework for assessment as a natural byproduct of the planning effort. Purpose, mission, desired effects, conditions, and tasks to subordinates represent goals for measuring progress. The assessment plan may be included in the coordinating instructions of the basic order. If it is complex, the plan could warrant its own tab, appendix, or separate annex. Planners must convey their situational understanding of the plan to the personnel working in current operations. This makes the planning process a learning activity and, with an intuitive level of understanding of the plan, the staff can shorten decision timelines significantly by immediately understanding the impact of change in the operational environment on the plan.

ASSESSMENT IN EXECUTION

During execution, assessment involves a deliberate comparison of forecasted outcomes to the current situation using criteria to judge progress toward the purpose. Commanders use it to increase their situational understanding and assess the operation in order to identify new opportunities and threats. Commanders maintain their situational understanding through a combination of personal observations and feedback from the staff and subordinate units. Feedback comes from all directions and in varying forms and degrees of maturity. The staff's role is to receive, analyze, correlate, synthesize, filter, and present information to the commander.

ASSESSMENT TOOLS

The Navy/Marine Corps Departmental Publication (NAVMC) 3500.97, *Marine Special Operations Command Training and Readiness (T&R) Manual*, is the primary assessment tool to evaluate MARSOF accomplishment of core mission-essential tasks. It establishes training standards, regulations, and practices for the training of Marines and assigned Navy personnel in MARFORSOC. The core capability mission-essential task list in NAVMC 3500.97 is used in the Defense Readiness Reporting System for the assessment and reporting of unit readiness. Units achieve training readiness by gaining and sustaining proficiency in the training events identified in NAVMC 3500.97 at both collective and individual levels. Commanders will use NAVMC 3500.97 to conduct internal assessments of a unit's ability to execute each mission-essential task and develop long-, mid-, and short-range training plans to sustain proficiency in each mission-essential task. Training plans will incorporate these events to standardize training and provide objective assessment of progress toward attaining combat readiness. Formal courses will use NAVMC 3500.97 to ensure programs of instruction meet skill training requirements in both execution and assessment of training.

This Page Intentionally Left Blank

GLOSSARY

Section I. Acronyms and Abbreviations

A&S .... assessment and selection
ADCON .... administrative control
AFO .... advance force operations
AOR .... area of responsibility

BLC .... Basic Language Course

C2 .... command and control
C4I .... command, control, communications, computers, and intelligence
C4ST .... command, control, communications, computers support team
CAO .... civil affairs operations
CCIR .... commander's critical information requirement
CDRJSOTF .... commander, joint special operations task force
CDRTSOC .... commander, theater special operations command
CDRUSSOCOM .... Commander, United States Special Operations Command
CJTF .... commander, joint task force
COIN .... counterinsurgency
COMMARFORSOC ....Commander, Marine Forces Special Operations Command
CSO .... critical skills operator
CSS .... combat service support
CWMD .... countering weapons of mass destruction

DOD .... Department of Defense
DOS .... Department of State
DST .... direct support team

EOD .... explosive ordnance disposal

F3EAD .... find, fix, finish, exploit, analyze, and disseminate
FID .... foreign internal defense
FSF .... foreign security forces

G-1 .... personnel staff section
G-2 .... intelligence staff section
G-3 .... operations staff section
G-4 .... logistics staff section
G-5 .... plans staff section
G-6 .... communications system staff section
G-7 .... training and education staff section

G-8 .... resource management staff section
G-9 .... recruiting and advertising staff section
GCC .... geographic combatant commander
GCTN .... global combating terrorism network

HN .... host nation
HQMC .... Headquarters, United States Marine Corps
HSS .... health service support

IDAD .... internal defense and development
ITC .... individual training course

JFC .... joint force commander
JFSOCC .... joint force special operations component commander
JP .... joint publication
JSOTF .... joint special operations task force
JTAC .... joint terminal attack controller
JTF .... joint task force

LST .... logistics support team

MAGTF .... Marine air-ground task force
MARFOR .... Marine Corps forces
MARFORSOC .... Marine Forces Special Operations Command
MARSOC .... United States Marine Corps Forces, Special Operations Command
MARSOF .... Marine special operations forces
MCDP .... Marine Corps doctrinal publication
MCRP .... Marine Corps reference publication
MCSOCOM DET .... Marine Corps United States Special Operations Command Detachment
                    (*Note*: MCSOCOM DET is used in historical context and is now obsolete.)
MCWP .... Marine Corps warfighting publication
MEU .... Marine expeditionary unit
MEU(SOC) .... Marine expeditionary unit (special operations capable)
          (*Note*: MEU[SOC] is used in historical context and is now obsolete, with no replacement.)
MISO .... military information support operations
MOE .... measure of effectiveness
MOP .... measure of performance
MOS .... military occupational specialty
MPC .... multi-purpose canine
MPOTFF .... MARFORSOC Preservation of the Force and Family
MSOC .... Marine special operations company
MSOS .... Marine Special Operations School
MSOT .... Marine special operations team

OPCON .... operational control
OSS .... Office of Strategic Services

rein .... reinforced

PE .... preparation of the environment
PME .... professional military education reinforced

S-1 .... personnel office
S-2 .... intelligence office
S-3 .... operations office
S-4 .... logistics office
S-6 .... communications office
SERE .... survival, evasion, resistance, and escape
SFA .... security force assistance
SOC-FWD .... special operations command-forward
SOCS .... special operations capability specialist
SOF .... special operations forces
SOFLE .... special operations forces liaison element
SOO .... special operations officer
SOR .... statement of requirement
SOTC .... special operations training company
SOTF .... special operations task force

TSOC .... theater special operations command
TTP .... tactics, techniques, and procedures

US .... United States
USG .... United States Government
USMC .... United States Marine Corps
USSOCOM .... United States Special Operations Command
UWOA .... unconventional warfare operating area

Section II. Terms

administrative control—Direction or exercise of authority over subordinate or other organizations in respect to administration and support. Also called **ADCON**. (JP 1-02)

antiterrorism—Defensive measures used to reduce the vulnerability of individuals and property to terrorist acts, to include rapid containment by local military and civilian forces. Also called **AT**. See also **counterterrorism**. (JP 1-02)

campaign—A series of related major operations aimed at achieving strategic and operational objectives within a given time and space. (JP 1-02)

campaign plan—A joint operation plan for a series of related major operations aimed at achieving strategic or operational objectives within a given time and space. (JP 1-02)

civil affairs—Designated Active and Reserve Component forces and units organized, trained, and equipped specifically to conduct civil affairs operations and to support civil-military operations. (JP 1-02)

civil affairs operations—Actions planned, executed, and assessed by civil affairs forces that enhance awareness of and manage the interaction with the civil component of the operational environment; identify and mitigate underlying causes of instability within civil society; or involve the application of functional specialty skills normally the responsibility of civil government. Also called **CAO**. (JP 1-02)

civil-military operations—Activities of a commander performed by designated civil affairs or other military forces that establish, maintain, influence, or exploit relations between military forces, indigenous populations, and institutions, by directly supporting the attainment of objectives relating to the reestablishment or maintenance of stability within a region or host nation. See also **civil affairs**; **operation**. (JP 1-02)

clandestine operation—An operation sponsored or conducted by governmental departments or agencies in such a way as to assure secrecy or concealment. See also **covert operation**. (JP 1-02)

coalition—An arrangement between two or more nations for common action. (JP 1-02)

combatant command—A unified or specified command with a broad continuing mission under a single commander established and so designated by the President, through the Secretary of Defense, and with the advice and assistance of the Chairman of the Joint Chiefs of Staff. (JP 1-02)

combatant command (command authority)—Nontransferable command authority, which cannot be delegated, of a combatant commander to perform those functions of command over assigned forces involving organizing and employing commands and forces; assigning tasks;

designating objectives; and giving authoritative direction over all aspects of military operations, joint training, and logistics necessary to accomplish the missions assigned to the command. Also called **COCOM**. See also **combatant command**; **operational control**; **tactical control**. (JP 1-02)

combating terrorism—Actions, including antiterrorism and counterterrorism, taken to oppose terrorism throughout the entire threat spectrum. (JP 1-02)

command relationships—The interrelated responsibilities between commanders, as well as the operational authority exercised by commanders in the chain of command; defined further as combatant command (command authority), operational control, tactical control, or support. See also **combatant command (command authority)**; **operational control**; **tactical control**. (JP 1-02)

conventional forces—(This is part two of a two-part definition.) Those forces other than designated special operations forces. (JP 1-02)

coordinating authority—A commander or individual who has the authority to require consultation between the specific functions or activities involving forces of two or more Services, joint force components, or forces of the same Service or agencies, but does not have the authority to compel agreement. (JP 1-02)

countering weapons of mass destruction—Efforts against actors of concern to curtail the conceptualization, development, possession, proliferation, use, and effects of weapons of mass destruction, related expertise, materials, technologies, and means of delivery. Also called **CWMD**. (JP 1-02)

counterinsurgency—Comprehensive civilian and military efforts designed to simultaneously defeat and contain insurgency and address its root causes. Also called **COIN**. (JP 1-02)

counterterrorism—Activities and operations taken to neutralize terrorists and their organizations and networks in order to render them incapable of using violence to instill fear and coerce governments or societies to achieve their goals. See also **antiterrorism**; **combating terrorism**; **terrorism**. (JP 1-02)

covert operation—An operation that is so planned and executed as to conceal the identity of or permit plausible denial by the sponsor. See also **clandestine operation**. (JP 1-02)

direct action—Short-duration strikes and other small-scale offensive actions conducted as a special operation in hostile, denied, or diplomatically sensitive environments and which employ specialized military capabilities to seize, destroy, capture, exploit, recover, or damage designated targets. See also **special operations**; **special operations forces**. (JP 1-02)

direct support—A mission requiring a force to support another specific force and authorizing it to answer directly to the supported force's request for assistance. See also **general support**. (JP 1-02)

foreign internal defense—Participation by civilian, military, and law enforcement agencies of a government in any of the action programs taken by another government or other designated organization to free and protect its society from subversion, lawlessness, insurgency, terrorism, and other threats to its security. Also called **FID**. (JP 1-02)

general support—(This is part one of a two part definition.) That support which is given to the supported force as a whole and not to any particular subdivision thereof. See also **direct support**. (JP 1-02)

guerrilla force—A group of irregular, predominantly indigenous personnel organized along military lines to conduct military and paramilitary operations in enemy-held, hostile, or denied territory. (JP 1-02)

information operations—(See JP 1-02 for core definition. Marine Corps amplification follows.) The integration, coordination, and synchronization of actions taken to affect a relevant decisionmaker in order to create an operational advantage for the commander. See also **military information support operations**. (MCRP 1-10.2)

insurgency—The organized use of subversion and violence to seize, nullify, or challenge political control of a region. Insurgency can also refer to the group itself. (JP 1-02)

intelligence operations—The variety of intelligence and counterintelligence tasks that are carried out by various intelligence organizations and activities within the intelligence process. (JP 1-02)

irregular warfare—A violent struggle among state and non-state actors for legitimacy and influence over the relevant populations(s). Also called **IW**. (JP 1-02)

joint force special operations component commander—The commander within a unified command, subordinate unified command, or joint task force responsible to the establishing commander for recommending the proper employment of assigned, attached, and/or made available for tasking special operations forces and assets; planning and coordinating special operations; or accomplishing such operational missions as may be assigned. Also called **JFSOCC**. (JP 1-02)

joint special operations area—An area of land, sea, and airspace assigned by a joint force commander to the commander of a joint special operations force to conduct special operations activities. (JP 1-02)

joint special operations task force—A joint task force composed of special operations units from more than one Service, formed to carry out a specific special operation or prosecute special operations in support of a theater campaign or other operations. Also called **JSOTF**. (JP 1-02)

joint task force—A joint force that is constituted and so designated by the Secretary of Defense, a combatant commander, a subunified commander, or an existing joint task force commander. Also called **JTF**. (JP 1-02)

Marine special operations forces—Those Active Component Marine Corps forces designated by the Secretary of Defense that are specifically organized, trained, and equipped to conduct and support special operations. Also called **MARSOF**. (Upon promulgation of this publication, this term and definition are approved for use and will be included in the next edition of MCRP 1-10.2.)

military information support operations—Planned operations to convey selected information and indicators to foreign audiences to influence their emotions, motives, objective reasoning, and ultimately the behavior of foreign governments, organizations, groups, and individuals in a manner favorable to the originator's objectives. Also called **MISO**. (JP 1-02)

mission type order—1. An order issued to a lower unit that includes the accomplishment of the total mission assigned to the higher headquarters. 2. An order to a unit to perform a mission without specifying how it is to be accomplished. (JP 1-02)

multinational—Between two or more forces or agencies of two or more nations or coalition partners. See also **coalition**. (JP 1-02)

multinational force—A force composed of military elements of nations who have formed an alliance or coalition for some specific purpose. (JP 1-02)

naval special warfare—A naval warfare specialty that conducts special operations with an emphasis on maritime, coastal, and riverine environments using small, flexible, mobile units operating under, on, and from the sea. (JP 1-02)

naval special warfare task group—A provisional naval special warfare organization that plans, conducts, and supports special operations in support of fleet commanders and joint force special operations component commanders. (JP 1-02)

nongovernmental organization—A private, self-governing, not-for-profit organization dedicated to alleviating human suffering; and/or promoting education, health care, economic development, environmental protection, human rights, and conflict resolution; and/or encouraging the establishment of democratic institutions and civil society. (JP 1-02)

operational control—The authority to perform those functions of command over subordinate forces involving organizing and employing commands and forces, assigning tasks, designating objectives, and giving authoritative direction necessary to accomplish the mission. Also called **OPCON**. See also **combatant command**; **combatant command (command authority)**; **tactical control**. (JP 1-02)

operational environment—A composite of the conditions, circumstances, and influences that affect the employment of capabilities and bear on the decisions of the commander. (JP 1-02)

preparation of the environment—An umbrella term for operations and activities conducted by selectively trained special operations forces to develop an environment for potential future special operations. Also called **PE**. (JP 1-02)

security assistance—Group of programs authorized by the Foreign Assistance Act of 1961, as amended, and the Arms Export Control Act of 1976, as amended, or other related statutes by which the United States provides defense articles, military training, and other defense-related services, by grant, loan, credit, or cash sales in furtherance of national policies and objectives. Security assistance is an element of security cooperation funded and authorized by Department of State to be administered by Department of Defense/Defense Security Cooperation Agency. (JP 1-02)

security cooperation—All Department of Defense interactions with foreign defense establishments to build defense relationships that promote specific US security interests, develop allied and friendly military capabilities for self-defense and multinational operations, and provide US forces with peacetime and contingency access to a host nation. (JP 1-02)

security force assistance—The Department of Defense activities that contribute to unified action by the US Government to support the development of the capacity and capability of foreign security forces and their supporting institutions. Also called **SFA**. (JP 1-02.)

security forces—Duly constituted military, paramilitary, police, and constabulary forces of a state. (JP 1-02.)

Service-common—Equipment, material, supplies, and services including base operating support adopted by a Service to support its own forces and those assigned to combatant commands; items and services defined as Service-common by one Service are not necessarily Service-common for all other Services. See also **special operations-peculiar**. (JP1-02)

special operations—Operations requiring unique modes of employment, tactical techniques, equipment and training often conducted in hostile, denied, or politically sensitive environments and characterized by one or more of the following: time sensitive, clandestine, low visibility, conducted with and/or through indigenous forces, requiring regional expertise, and/or a high degree of risk. (JP 1-02)

special operations forces—Those Active and Reserve Component forces of the Services designated by the Secretary of Defense and specifically organized, trained, and equipped to conduct and support special operations. Also called **SOF**. (JP 1-02)

special operations joint task force—A modular, tailorable, and scalable special operations task force designed to provide integrated, fully-capable, and enabled joint special operations forces to geographic combatant commanders and joint force commanders. (JP 1-02)

special operations-peculiar—Equipment, material, supplies, and services required for special operations missions for which there is no Service-common requirement. See also **Service-common**; **special operations**. (JP 1-02)

special reconnaissance—Reconnaissance and surveillance actions conducted as a special operation in hostile, denied, or diplomatically and/or politically sensitive environments to collect or verify information of strategic or operational significance, employing military capabilities not normally found in conventional forces. Also called **SR**. (JP 1-02)

stability operations—An overarching term encompassing various military missions, tasks, and activities conducted outside the United States in coordination with other instruments of national power to maintain or reestablish a safe and secure environment, provide essential governmental services, emergency infrastructure reconstruction, and humanitarian relief. (JP 1-02)

tactical control—The authority over forces that is limited to the detailed direction and control of movements or maneuvers within the operational area necessary to accomplish missions or tasks assigned. See also **combatant command**; **combatant command (command authority)**; **operational control**. (JP 1-02)

targeting—The process of selecting and prioritizing targets and matching the appropriate response to them, considering operational requirements and capabilities. (JP 1-02)

terrorism—The unlawful use of violence or threat of violence, often motivated by religious, political, or other ideological beliefs, to instill fear and coerce governments or societies in pursuit of goals that are usually political. See also **antiterrorism**; **combating terrorism**; **counterterrorism**. (JP 1-02)

theater special operations command—A subordinate unified command established by a combatant commander to plan, coordinate, conduct, and support joint special operations. Also called **TSOC**. See also **special operations**. (JP 1-02)

unconventional warfare—Activities conducted to enable a resistance movement or insurgency to coerce, disrupt, or overthrow a government or occupying power by operating through or with an underground, auxiliary, and guerrilla force in a denied area. (JP 1-02)

unified action—The synchronization, coordination, and/or integration of the activities of governmental and nongovernmental entities with military operations to achieve unity of effort. (JP 1-02)

weapons of mass destruction—Chemical, biological, radiological, or nuclear weapons capable of a high order of destruction or causing mass casualties, and excluding the means of transporting or propelling the weapon where such means is a separable and divisible part from the weapon. Also called **WMD**. See also **special operations**. (JP 1-02)

This Page Intentionally Left Blank

REFERENCES AND RELATED PUBLICATIONS

Office of the Secretary of Defense Publication

Guidance for Employment of the Force 2015–2017 (Publication is SECRET)

Department of Defense Publications

Joint Operating Concept for Irregular Warfare: Countering Irregular Threats v2.0
The National Military Strategy of the United States of America 2015
Quadrennial Defense Review 2014

Joint Publications (JPs)

1-02	Department of Defense Dictionary of Military and Associated Terms
3-05	Special Operations
3-05.1	Unconventional Warfare
3-24	Counterinsurgency
3-26	Counterterrorism

Allied Joint Publication (AJP)

AJP-3.5   Allied Joint Doctrine for Special Operations

Army Publications

Army Doctrine Reference Publication (ADRP)
3-05   Special Operations

United States Army War College (USAWC) publication
Clark, Mark A. (Lt. Col.). *USAWC Strategy Research Project: Should the Marine Corps Expand its Role in Special Operations?*, Carlisle, PA: U.S. Army War College, 2003.

Marine Corps Publications

Marine Corps Doctrinal Publication (MCDPs)
1   Warfighting
1-0   Marine Corps Operations

Marine Corps Warfighting Publications (MCWPs)
3-02   Insurgencies and Countering Insurgencies

Marine Corps Reference Publications (MCRPs)
1-10.1   Organization of the United States Marine Corps
3-30.4   Multi-Service Tactics, Techniques, and Procedures for Conventional
                     Forces and Special Operations Forces Integration, Interoperability, and
                     Interdependence (CFSOF)

Marine Corps Orders (MCOs)
1200.18   Military Occupational Specialties (MOS) Program Order
1500.53_   Marine Air-Ground Task Force Staff Training Program

Navy/Marine Corps Departmental Publication (NAVMC)
3500.97   Marine Special Operations Command Training and Readiness Manual

Fleet Marine Force Reference Publication (FMFRP)
12-15   Small Wars Manual

U.S. Marine Corps Forces, Special Operations Command Order (MARSOCO)
2201   U.S. Marine Corps Forces, Special Operations Command Doctrine Program

Miscellaneous
Mattingly, Robert E. (Maj). *Herringbone Cloak—G.I. Dagger Marines of the OSS* (Washington, DC: Headquarters, U.S. Marine Corps, History and Museums Division, 1989).

Marine Corps Concepts and Programs April 2016

Marine Corps Operating Concepts for a Changing Security Environment

United States Marine Corps Expeditionary Force 21

Systems Approach to Training (SAT) Manual (June 2004)

Updegraph, Charles L., Jr. *Special Marine Corps Units of World War II* (Washington, DC: Headquarters, U.S. Marine Corps, History and Museums Division, 1972).

Navy Publications

Navy Concept
Naval Operations Concept 2010

<u>Navy Warfare Publication (NWP)</u>
3-05   Naval Special Warfare

United States Special Operations Command (USSOCOM) Publications

Capabilities and Programming Guidance (2017–2021)

Commander's Memorandum for Education and Training Guidance, FY 2013–2016

Directive 10-1cc, Terms of Reference–Roles, Missions, and Functions of Component Commands

Directive 350-1, USSOCOM Military Training

Joint SOF Doctrine Campaign Plan for FY 2014–2015

Publication 1, Doctrine for Special Operations

Multi-Service Concept for Irregular Warfare August 2006

US Congress, House, House Armed Services Committee. *Posture Statement of Admiral William H. McRaven, USN, Commander, United States Special Operations Command.* 113th Cong., 5 March 2013.

Other Publications

Lacey, Laura Hoffman. *Ortiz: To Live a Man's Life*, 2nd Edition, Williamstown, N.J.: Phillips Publications, 2012.

This Page Intentionally Left Blank

Made in the USA
Columbia, SC
16 August 2024

40270330R00063